CYPRUS

CYPRUS

Series editor
Michael Shichor

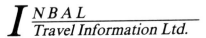

Inbal Travel Information Ltd.
P.O.Box 39090 Tel Aviv Israel 61390

©1992 edition

Intl. ISBN 965-288-030-2

Text: Yoram Ya'accobi

Distributed in Cyprus by:
N.G. Triarchos & Co. Ltd.
14 Kantaras Avenue
Kaimakhi
Nicosia

Distributed in the United Kingdom by:
Kuperard (London) Ltd.
9, Hampstead West
224 Iverson Road
West Hampstead
London NW6 2HL

U.K. ISBN 1-870668-54-5

CONTENTS

Preface   **11**
Using this Guide   **12**

INTRODUCTION   15

Part One — Getting to Know Cyprus   **16**
A long history in brief (16), Geography and climate (22),
The People (24), Economy (25), Byzantine and Gothic
architecture (26)

Part Two — Setting Out   **29**
How to get there (29), Documents (30), Customs (31), When
to travel (31), Holidays (31), How long to stay (33), How much
will it cost (33), What to wear (34)

Part Three — Easing the Shock   **35**
Getting around (35), Public transportation (35), Organized
tours (37), Accommodation (38), Food and restaurants (39),
Tourist information (42), Sport (43), Shopping (43), General
information (44), Visiting Cyprus — step by step (47)

CYPRUS   53

Larnaca   **53**
How to get there (53), Tourist services (55), Accommodation
(56), Restaurants (59), What to see (60), The Salt Lake (63),
Pyla (64)

Agia Napa   65
From Larnaca to Limassol   75

Limassol   **79**
How to get there (79), Urban transportation (80), Tourist
services (80), Accommodation (81), Restaurants (84),
Shopping (85), What to see (85), Night life (87), The Limassol
District (88), From Limassol to Pafos (89)

Pafos   95
How to get there (96), Tourist services (96), Accommodation
(97), Restaurants (100), Shopping (100), Transportation (100),
What to see (101), Around Pafos (107), From Pafos to Troodos
(109)

The Troodos Mountains   112
Mountain walks   121
From Troodos to Nicosia   123

Nicosia   125
The City Structure (128), How to get there (128), Tourist
services (130), Accommodation (132), Restaurants (133),
Shopping (134), Sports (136), What to see (137), Around
Nicosia (140)

Turkish Cyprus   143
Lefkosa — Turkish Nicosia (143), The western tour (145), The
eastern tour (153)

*I*NDEX   159

*N*OTES   163

*T*ABLE OF MAPS

Cyprus   50
Larnaca   58
Agia Napa   66
Limassol   82
Pafos   98
Around Pafos   110
The Troodos Mountains   114
Nicosia   126

Preface

Cyprus, the majestic island in the eastern Mediterranean, acts as a mirror reflecting the historical vagaries of this part of the world — from the Egyptians to the Persians, and from the Romans to the Byzantine Empire. Its diversed and complicated history is reflected in the unsolved conflict between the Greek and Turkish populations living on the island — each contributing to its character and beauty.

Many Europeans find Cyprus an ideal holiday destination. It is blessed with beautiful beaches and moderate temperament, typical of its weather and people, as is appropriate to a Mediterranean island. What's more, the fast development of its infrastructure promises visitors a pleasant and convenient holiday.

We have devoted the major part of this guide to Greek Cyprus. Since the partition of the Island in 1974, the Greek part, which accounts for two thirds of the entire island, has enjoyed accelerated economic and tourist development, and most tourists visiting the island visit this part. The Turkish side, on the other hand, has an inadequate infrastructure and can cater primarily to day-trippers residing on the Greek side of the island. At the end of the guide you'll find a special chapter devoted to visitors wishing to take excursions to the Turkish side.

We trust that with our guide's help you'll discover a Cyprus beyond beaches and hotels, a Cyprus rich in history, a Cyprus of mountains dotted with monasteries and forests, villages and hamlets. We hope that you will experience Cyprus as an island of peace and quiet in a raging sea of modern pulsating life.

Michael Shichor

Using this Guide

In order to use this Guide in the most efficient way, we recommend that you read the following advice and act upon it.

The Guide includes a great deal of data meant to help you find your way and ensure that you see as much as possible with maximum saving of time, money and effort.

Before setting out, read the Introduction in its entirety. It provides the essential information you will need to know and understand before making the advance arrangements for your trip. Reviewing the material thoroughly, and acting upon it, means that you will be better organized and prepared for your visit.

The basic guideline in all of "MICHAEL'S GUIDE" publications is to survey places primarily in geographical sequence and not a thematic one. A geographical plan not only ensures the most efficient use of time, but also contributes dramatically to getting to know an area in its different aspects and acquiring a feel for it. Furthermore, you will be directed from a museum to a recommended restaurant or entertainment place, incorporating in your visit to one site several other locations which you may not have thought or heard of beforehand.

The chapters on main towns include maps and indexes of sites that will help you find out your way. On reaching each town, the Guide will direct you to recommended accommodation and restaurants. The maps will assist you in getting from one place to another.

There is a detailed index of all the places and sites covered in the Guide, at the end of the book.

At press time, information contained in this Guide was correct, but it is possible that you may discover certain inaccuracies due to unforeseen changes, and for that we apologise.

It is crucial that you check local information as much as possible when you actually arrive in Cyprus. A good source of information is your hotel reception or local office of the CTO (Cyprus Tourism Organisation). Most towns have an information office open during the summer season and details are given under the appropriate sections.

In order to keep ourselves updated, we are in need of your help. The cooperation of those who enjoyed what this Guide has to offer is essential, and ensures that those who follow you, will have as much accurate information at their disposal as you did. For this purpose we have included a short questionnaire at the end and would be grateful, if you were to answer in and return it to us.

Have a good and enjoyable trip!

*I*NTRODUCTION

Cyprus — the birthplace of Venus; the first overseas step of many an ancient wanderer, hailing from Greece or Turkey, from Egypt or Syria; the battle ground of so many gods: Assyrian and Egyptian, Persian and Roman, Christian and Moslem... for more than forty centuries. All its visitors, conquerors and looters of past centuries left the imprint of their loves and hates, their dreams and fears, their happiness and tears on that little island.

You will not witness the rebirth of Venus. You will not hear the crusaders trumpets embarking toward the Holy Land. And you will not see the blood and tears of Othello and Desdemona...

Yet, you will enjoy a splendid array of beaches; modern and inexpensive hotels, just a few miles from a backdrop of medieval hamlets; some of the most famous wines in history; pine forests and olive groves and lots of ancient vineyards; ruins of forts and temples, monasteries and churches, baths and theatres...

You will enjoy a unique atmosphere, of mixed east and west, of mingled pride and patience, of legendary history and of historic legend...

*I*NTRODUCTION

Part One — Getting to Know Cyprus

A Long History in Brief

The history of Cyprus begins almost eight thousands years ago. All the early seafaring peoples of the eastern Mediterranean left their mark on the island: ancient Egypt and Greece, Alexander the Great, the Phoenicians, the Assyrians, Persia, Rome, the Byzantine Empire, the Crusaders, Venice, the Ottomans, the British — all these and more conquered and ruled the island and its people over the centuries. Having finally won its independence, in 1974 Cyprus found itself, after a brief but cruel civil war, divided in two, with the northern region affiliated to Turkey and the southern region to Greece.

Ancient Times

The earliest signs of human settlement date from the Neolithic Period, in the sixth millennium BC. Remnants are found in several hamlets in an area of watercourses and springs; the most ancient is Choirokoitia, halfway between Nicosia and Limassol. Findings of imported stoneware objects clearly point to trade contacts with the Anatolian population. The earthenware and copper objects discovered in Erimi (near Limassol) and in Souskiou (near Pafos) date from the **Chalcolithic Period** (3rd millennium BC).

During the **Bronze Age** (2300-1800 BC), the Cypriots farmed the land, worshipped a Fertility God (in bull shape) and a Death God (symbolized by a snake); this points again to their ties with overseas neighbours in Egypt and in Asia Minor.

The **Middle Bronze Age** (1800-1600 AC) is best represented in Eastern Cyprus (in Kalopsida); during this period Cyprus also came into close contact with the Greek Islands.

During the **Late Bronze Age** (1600-1050 AC) the Mycaenean culture swept the Aegean Sea, reached and conquered Cyprus, settling along its eastern and southern shores and building several new towns and harbours. The discovery of rich copper mines provided Cyprus with new wealth and enabled it to buy peace from its more powerful neighbours by means of copper tributes, paid to the Egyptian Kings.

Toward the end of the 13th century BC many hamlets began to grow into small towns, complete with walls, temples and public buildings; Greek customs and culture were slowly adopted throughout the island.

At the beginning of the 1st millennium BC a terrible earthquake shook the island and razed all its cities. It was only centuries later that the ancient centres were slowly rebuilt, often with new names. During this period (the **Iron Age**) the Phoenicians settled along the southern plain; their presence is documented by the ruins of a great temple to their goddess Astarte.

The Assyrian, Egyptian and Roman Rule

The Assyrians conquered Cyprus in 709 BC and held it until 560 BC, when they were defeated and ousted by the Egyptians. The conquerors left the local Cypriot kings in power, demanding an annual tribute in gold and copper. When Cyprus fell into the Persian Empire sphere of influence (525 BC), the local kings were again allowed to remain in power, as long as taxes and tributes continued to flow. The fiscal yoke was so heavy that the Cypriots staged several rebellions, repeatedly repressed with cruelty. However, Cyprus' independent spirit survived, and its folk zealously maintained their Greek cultural orientation.

In 333 BC the island was conquered by Alexander the Great. In 294, after his death, Cyprus was annexed to Egypt by Ptolomeus I, who ruled Cyprus through an appointed Governor. Cyprus became independent in 109 BC, when Ptolomeus IX, threatened by his mother Cleopatras, was forced to flee Egypt, thus appointing himself the King of Cyprus. Rome put an end to the . Ptolomaean rule in 58 BC, and under the legendary "Pax Romana" Cyprus enjoyed a new period of peace and prosperity, as witnessed by the ruins of several highways, aqueducts and theatres.

St. Paul brought the message of Christiendom to Cyprus; the Roman Governor Sergius had him lashed and flagellated, but ended up by embracing the new faith himself. Paul set up ten bishopries in the main towns. The local church was headed by the Archbishop of Salamis. In 331 Cyprus became a province of the Byzantine Empire within the Antiochian administration. The local Church, however, maintained its autonomy. .

In the 6th Century Cyprus became dependent upon Constantinople; under Justinianus' rule, Cyprus enjoyed a new wave of prosperity, as witnessed by the many beautiful mosaics whose remnants can still be admired.

The Islamic-Byzantine Conflict
When Islam began to spread throughout the southern shores of the Mediterranean, Byzantine Cyprus was doomed. In 647 the Caliph of Baghdad imposed new taxes and tributes, and a few years later an Arab Praesidium was set up on the island. The conflict continued for about three centuries, with several invasions from north and south.

In 965 the Byzantine Emperor, Nicaphoros, conquered the island establishing it as his front against the Islam. The Crusaders landed in Cyprus to prepare themselves for the last leg of their journey. Christianity launched its campaigns against Antiochia and Tripoli (Syria) from Cyprus. Time after time the Syrians retaliated, destroying the land and slaughtering its people. In 1191 Richard the Lionheart, at the head of the third Crusade, conquered

Cyprus almost overnight. Today's major centres, Nicosia, Limassol and Famagusta, date from his time.

The Lusignan Dynasty

Richard gave Cyprus to Guy de Lusignan, a French nobleman who aspired to the crown of Jerusalem. Three years later, in 1194, Guy died and his brother Aimery took over the newly founded feudal Kingdom of Cyprus, swearing allegiance to the German Holy Roman Empire. All lands and properties of the Greek Orthodox Church were confiscated in favour of the Catholic Church.

The Greek peasants of Cyprus lived in great poverty, deprived of freedom. During the next century Cyprus remained a faithful ally of the Kingdom of Jerusalem, and served as the Crusades' main strategic base.

After a period of strife and rebellion, Cyprus once again made a quick recovery, becoming one of the most prosperous trade centres of the Eastern Mediterranean, exporting silk, sugar and spices to Europe. New, imposing Gothic Cathedrals were built in Famagusta, Nicosia and elsewhere.

The Lusignan Dynasty ended in 1369, with the murder of King Pierre at the hands of his barons, and for the next century Cyprus passed from one conquerer to the next. Genoa conquered it, Egypt sacked it. Thanks to an alliance between James II and the Venetian Doges, for close to a century the island became a Venetian fief. Venetian palaces lined the main streets of Famagusta and St. Mark's Lion stood at the entrance of all Cyprus' main seaports.

After a long struggle for eastern trade between Venice and the Ottoman Empire, Venice was finally defeated and Cyprus fell into Ottoman hands in 1575.

The Ottoman Rule

The new rulers brought the Greek Orthodox Church back to Cyprus; the Orthodox Archbishop was also appointed

Head of State. Feudal servitude was abolished, but the heavy taxes imposed on farmers and peasants did little to improve their former condition.

The next two centuries were an epoch of great poverty, drought and pestilence. Frequent rebellions were quelled by the Ottoman rulers, who did not hesitate to execute even the Archbishop himself. Turkish soldiers were granted lands confiscated from the rebels (sowing the seeds of the local Greek-Turkish conflict, which in the 1970s' culminated in civil war — and the subsequent partition of Cyprus).

In 1878 Turkey signed an agreement, granting Cyprus to Great Britain, in return for British support against Russia.

British Rule
In 1914 Cyprus was officially granted the status of a Crown Colony, and as such became involved in the First World War, at the side of Great Britain, France, Italy and later the United States. In 1915 Great Britain offered Cyprus to Greece, on condition that Greece join the Allies. But Greece joined the fighting only in 1917, and after the war the Allies found reason not to honour their pledge.

For the Cypriots, however, annexation to Greece had become the dream of "Enosis", and the British were repeatedly forced to use arms to repress the frequent rebellions.

During the Second World War, several thousand Cypriots served in the British Army; others found themselves fighting the Nazi invaders from the peaks of Cyprus' mountains. In 1950, after a new wave of "Enosis" strife, the annexation to Greece was finally sanctioned by plebiscite. Greece attempted to force implementation of the vote at the United Nations, but Great Britain and Turkey stalled the issue.

In 1955 Colonel Grivas, a Cyprus born colonel in the Greek Army, founded the EOKA, a sort of "People's Army for Enosis", and Archbishop Makarios gave Enosis his full support. The London Conference, held some weeks later, in which London, Athens and Ankara sought a mutually acceptable solution , ended in failure. The relations between Greece and Turkey became extremely strained. In 1956 the Suez crisis provided Britain with justification to strengthen its local garrison.

Martial law was declared; Makarios and his deputy were deported to the Seychelles Islands. In 1957 they were pardoned, in exchange for an EOKA declaration of ceasefire. EOKA, however, resumed the fight barely one year later.

On 11 February 1959, when it became apparent that Enosis could not be wiped out, Great Britain, Turkey and Greece, joined in conference at Zurich, finally granted Cyprus its independence.

Independence

On 16 August 1960, Cyprus officially declared its independence within the British Commonwealth. The Turkish minority (about 18% of the population) was granted a 30% representation in Parliament and in the Administration, as well as 40% of the Armed Forces and the office of Deputy President, with rights of veto. Great Britain was allowed to maintain its naval bases, in return for its pledge to guarantee Cyprus' independence.

The apparent honeymoon only lasted for a few years. The cumbersome structure of the administration, with its dual foundations, caused renewed strife. In 1963 the parties came to blows, which grew into a full scale civil war, and ended only with the intervention of a United Nations peace force. The peacemakers set up a dividing line between Greeks and Turks, cutting the capital Nicosia in two. This line became the border of two separate political entities: Greek Cyprus and Turkish Cyprus.

The two parent States repeatedly found themselves on the brink of war. The central administration lost its power. The Turkish representatives abandoned their Parliamentary seats and the Deputy President resigned.

I<u>NTRODUCTION</u>

When a military junta overthrew the democratic government of Greece, a rift also appeared among Cypriot' Greeks. Archbishop Makarios supported democracy; Grivas favoured the junta. The Archbishop's followers took up arms against Grivas' troops.

War and Partition
In 1974 a coup brought the extreme right to power, supported by units of the Greek Army. Makarios was ousted; the new president, Nikos Sampson, lasted less than a week. His successor, Glafkos Clerides, was not recognized by the Turks, whose army invaded the island from the north, conquering one third of its territory, to the Morphou-Nicosia-Famagusta line (the so-called Attila Line). A ceasefire was declared; 200,000 Greeks, residents of the Turkish zone, crossed the line toward the west, and the Turks living in the Greek zone crossed in the opposite direction. The Turkish zone unilaterally declared its own independence.

The situation today is practically the same as it was in 1975. The Western Zone calls itself (in Greek) Kipriaki Democratia; the Eastern Zone calls itself the Turkish Republic of Northern Cyprus (in Turkish Kuzey Kibris Türk Cumhuriyeti). Each side has its own President, Parliament and Cabinet. There are no ties whatsoever between the two.

In official maps published by the two sides, the same localities have different names: Greek Famagusta appears, in Turkish maps, as Gazi Maguza; Nicosia appears as Lefkoza — and so on.

Geography
Cyprus is an island in the Eastern Mediterranean, 40 miles south of Turkey and 60 miles west of Syria. Cyprus is the third largest island in the Mediterranean, after Sicily and Sardinia. It covers an area of 3,572 square miles; its maximum east-west spread is 128 miles; north-south 75 miles. Its shores run along about 450 miles.

INTRODUCTION

The island is of Myocenic tectonic origin, separated in the epoch of Asia Minor and the Peloponesian islands.

Its origins are reflected in its three main regions: the Troodos Mountains in the West, the Central Mesaoria Plain and the Northern Chain of the Kyrenia Mountains. The Kyrenia Plain in the North, and the hills of the Coastal Plain in the South, complete the geographic structure of the island.

The **Troodos Mountains** cover the south-western quadrant of the island, and are vulcanic in character. Its highest peak, Mt. Olympus, soars to a height of 6,403 feet. The chain covers an area of close to 1000 square miles.

Its northern, granitic ridge is steep and barren; its southern hills are calcareous in nature, and crisscrossed by a net of seasonal waterbeds. The main divide runs from east to west.

Northern Troodos farming is limited to small lots and parcels. Extensive vineyards and orchards are only found on the slopes of the southern hills. The main industrial branch is tourism; the summer climate is pleasantly cool, and in winter the slopes offer some adequate ski runs.

The **Mesaoria Plain** is the heart of Cyprus. Wide, fertile farmland covers the Troodos foothills in the south and the Kyrenia range in the north, and down to the eastern and western Mediterranean beaches. The main river of Cyprus, the Pedieos, crosses the plain from south-west to north-east, providing farmers with ample irrigation water. The main agricultural produce is grain and citrus plantations.

Four of the six major urban centres of Cyprus — Nicosia, Limassol, Larnaca and Famagusta — are in Mesaoria. Cyprus' international airport is based in Larnaca; Limassol and Famagusta are two deep-water harbours, frequented by hundreds of ships, and Nicosia is the seat of government, and the largest town on the island.

The **Northern Coastal Plain** is a narrow strip running from

Cape Kormakitis eastward to Cape Andreas, between the Kyrenia Range and the sea. It is about 90 miles long, and no less than 3 miles wide. The island ends with the pointing finger of the Karpas Peninsula at the far east.

The **Kyrenia Mountains**, or Besparmak (Mounts of the Five Fingers), separate the Coastal Plain from the Mesaoria. Their northern slopes are covered with pine forests; the southern side is almost utterly barren. The slopes of the Karpas Peninsula are a scrubland, rich of wild olive bushes; the soil is too thin and poor for anything but carob and olive trees. Along the beaches you may find some modest lemon and fruit groves.

Climate
Cyprus enjoys a very pleasant climate. However, July and August are rather hot, and may reach even 100 F. (86 F. in the mountains). Nights are much cooler. In winter, even in the mountains the temperature seldom reaches 35F; in the coastal plains 40-60 F. and inland slighly less.

The average annual rainfall reaches about 16 inches in the coastal plains, 12 inches inland, and 30 inches in the mountains; the rainy season — winter — lasts no longer than 80 days.

Seawater temperature ranges from 50 F. in winter to 80 F. in summer; water content is poor in salts and minerals, resulting in its vivid blue colour.

The People
Cyprus has a population of about 700,000 people, subdivided into two main groups: the Greek majority, and the Turkish minority. The Greeks represent the original population of the island; the Turkish minority dates from the Ottoman rule (1571-1878), when the administration granted land confiscated from its original Greek owners to members of the Turkish garrison.

77% of the population are Christian Orthodox, 18%

Moslem, and the rest are Catholic, Maron and Armenian Christians.

As soon as you leave the main roads, you will find yourself in another world: at few miles from the westernized modern towns, with their luxury hotels and high-rises, you will come across crumbling hamlets and isolated farms. Along the roads you will meet shepherds and labourers that seem to belong to times gone by.

The Languages
The two local languages are, of course, Greek and Turkish, but English is also widely spoken. There are several weeklies and one daily newspaper in English; day old copies of foreign dailies are available at the main newsstands in all major cities. The local radio stations and the single TV channel broadcast daily programmes in English.

Learning Greek in Cyprus
Several modern institutes offer courses in spoken modern Greek: for further information, call the Governmental Institute at tel. 02-302023, 02-303140 or 02-402682, or private institutes at 02-445970, 02-459501 or 02-421970 — all in Nicosia. The Institutes have branches in Limassol, Larnaka and Pafos. For further details, call the CTO.

Economy
During the 60's Cyprus enjoyed a period of prosperity, which ended with the 1973 drought and the 1974 civil war. The partition disrupted all economic ties between the sectors. The Greek side was able to make a fast comeback, and today there is practically no unemployment, and the financial situation is stable. The Turkish sector is still rather backward, with high unemployment and very low standards of living. The information below refers to the economy of the Greek sector.

Agriculture employs one third of the labour force, and its income amounts to 20% of the GNP. Grain is widely grown (25% of the total agricultural output), mainly for local consumption; some of the other products are potatoes, grapes, citruses, vegetables and milk — mainly for export. Sheep farming is also common, particularly in natural pastures on the hills.

Minerals were formerly Cyprus' main resource; today they amount to very little: almost all mines are in the northern — Turkish — zone; prices are low and the ore is poor.

Industry employs about 25% of the labour force, mainly in small private plants producing consumer goods and foodstuff, especially tobacco and wine for export.

Almost half the labour force is employed in **Public Services** — banks, transportation and tourism.

Tourism is Cyprus' major source of foreign currency. In 1990 more than 1.5 million tourists visited the island, bringing in more than one billion US$. In fact, Cyprus, with its 700,000 people, has ample facilities for four times as many tourists, with dozens of new hotels, sites and activities.

In spite of this, the economy of Cyprus is still in the red: it exports wine, potatoes, copper and citruses to Europe and imports raw materials, fuel, grain and consumer goods from Europe, the USA and Japan.

Byzantine and Gothic Architecture

Most churches and monasteries in Cyprus are in Byzantine or Gothic style.

During the Byzantine Era, starting with the 4th Century AD, even the smaller centres had their own basilica, with its characteristic elongated nave and atrium. Today, however, none of these remain.

What remains are shards of mosaic floors, the remnants of centuries of religious wars. Perhaps the most interesting is at Angeloktistos, a small village not far from Larnaca. This mosaic depicts the Virgin Mary holding the Infant in her arms, with two Archangels — Gabriel and Michael — at her sides. More about Cyprus' mosaics will be mentioned in the following chapters.

Other fragments have been recovered at Lambousa, near Kyrenia, in the Turkish zone, and are housed at the **Cyprus Museum** in Nicosia and in the British Museum, in London.

The five-domed basilicas, such as Geroskipou (near Pafos) or Peristerona, are later structures developed from earlier, three-domed models such as those at **St. Barnabas** in New Salamis or **St. Lazaros** in Larnaca.

Later Byzantine structures are often decorated with fresco paintings, often modelled on similar works of art common in 11th and 12th century Constantinople. Shards of such frescoes can be seen in St. Nicholas of Kakopetria and in the Asinoa Church (both high in the mountains) and in some other sites as well.

The Lusignan reign introduced Cyprus to the Gothic style. Gothic churches and cathedrals were built in Kyrenia, in Pyrga and in Famagusta. These were almost exact copies of contemporary churches in Northern France, home of the de Lusignans. Later, during the 14th Century, the architects of Cyprus were inspired by Southern French churches. At the Moutoullas mountain church, which dates from the same period, the influence of oriental schools of religious art is evident in the frescoes.

From the beginning of the 15th century, Venice became the major influence, both in architectural structure and in interior decoration (see the Galata Church, 1502). The Gothic style, however, did not disappear from the Cyprus scene, it is represented, for instance, in 16th and 17th Century buildings, such as Bedestan and St. Dhometios in Nicosia, and the Archangellos Monastery at Lakatamia.

Arts and Crafts
The handicraft of Cyprus has been famous for centuries. King Agamemnon received a splendid golden mail from Cyprus; Alexander the Great's famous sword also hailed

*I*NTRODUCTION

from Cyprus. Cyprus' handicrafts can be admired at the National Museum and at the Folklore Museum of Nicosia.

The *Cyprus Handicraft Service* (25 Demophontos St., Nicosia), provides interested tourists with a list of specialized original handicraft outlets throughout the island.

*I*NTRODUCTION

Part Two — Setting Out

How to get there

By Air

Several European and Middle Eastern Airlines connect Larnaca's Airport with most European Capitals. The National Tender, *Air Cyprus* (21 Alkaeus St., POB 1903, Nicosia, tel. 02-443054; booking office 50 Makarios Ave., tel. 02-441996) offers several weekly flights to Athens, Rome, Paris, London, Manchester, Birmingham, Munich, Zurich, Geneva and other cities.

During the high season, dozens of additional charter flights connect Cyprus with Europe, and especially Great Britain, Germany and Scandinavia. Such flights often land at Pafos' Airport, comfortably close to some of the best seaside resorts.

The Turkish zone (the Turkish Republic of Northern Cyprus) has no direct airway connections with Europe. The only way is to catch a flight to Ankara, Istanbul, Adana or Antalia (in Turkey) and transfer to a local flight of the *Cyprus Turkish Airline* (*KTHY*), whose main office is situated in Turkish Nicosia (28 Bedreddin Demirel Ave., tel. 520-71901, telex 57350 YKKC TK). The London Office of *KTHY* is at 28 Cockspur St., tel. 01-9304851; the Istanbul Office is at the Sheraton Hotel, tel. 141-5732 or 141-7674).

By Sea

Several shipping lines frequent Cyprus' main harbours, connecting the island with Italy, Greece, Israel, Lebanon, Egypt, Syria, Turkey etc. Of course, if the flight-time to Cyprus, from Europe, is 4-5 hours at the most, a cruise in the Mediterranean may take longer than a week before reaching the island.

The seafares vary according to a very simple scale: you may travel on deck (for less than half the price of an airflight) and you may travel in a luxury stateroom, enjoying the luxury of a five-star hotel — and pay accordingly...

Your travel agent will probably be able to inform you of all Mediterranean cruises and shipping lines available, their timetables and their prices.

People of leisure may reach Cyprus by (hired or private) yacht. Cyprus has as many as five Yachting Clubs: two in Larnaca, two in Limassol and one in Pafos. Often, on a single day, you will see over two hundred yachts moored at the Larnaca Marina — hailing from all the major European ports and even from farther out.

In the Turkish zone, a regular line connects Kyrenia with the port of Mersin (in south-eastern Turkey); both Kyrenia and Famagusta have adequate facilities for visiting yachts.

Crossing the line between the two zones
Tourists attempting to cross the line from Greek Cyprus to the Turkish zone should be prepared for all sorts of delays and even abuse; crossing in the opposite direction is simply out of the question.

The only crossing points are at the Nicosia gates.

Documents
Foreigners need a valid passport or other official documents confirming national identity in order to enter Cyprus as a tourist. Your agent will certainly know whether a visa is necessary, and in that case he will be able to assist you in obtaining it. At the entrance gate, officials may inquire whether visitors possess sufficient funds to cover their stay (at least 30 $US per diem).

If you want to drive a vehicle, be sure to obtain an international driver's licence with an identifying photograph.

Health insurance, as it is everywhere else in the world,

is a must; it is also convenient to insure your effects and luggage.

Customs

Cyprus laws exempt tourists from payment of customs for up to 200 cigarettes, one liter of liquor, one bottle of wine and 300 cc. of perfume.

You may bring in (and take out) up to 50 Cyprus pounds, and unlimited foreign currency. The laws state that sums exceeding $US 1,000 should be declared on entrance, but this law is not usually observed. You may bring in a vehicle and a boat — but you will not be allowed to hire them out or to sell them. The *Green Insurance Card*, valid in Europe is not valid in Cyprus, but at most ports of entry you may purchase short term insurance policies for your vehicle and other effects.

For additional information contact the Nicosia Customs Authority, tel. 02-303175.

When to Travel

We have already described the local climate. The ideal seasons are spring and autumn, when temperatures are most comfortable, the weather is dry and the tourist resorts are seldom overcrowded. In the high season (July and August) you will be well advised to reserve your accommodation in advance, perhaps through your travel agent. Most resorts and beaches will also be crowded.

Holidays

The following list includes general holidays as well as local festivals, religious and otherwise, held in various towns and villages.

1 January — New Year. Housewives bake a traditional loaf, called *Vasilopitta*, with a coin hidden inside it for good luck.

6 January — Epiphany. In the coastal towns, the priests throw a holy cross into the sea, and the most daring and courageous youngsters dive in to retrieve it.

INTRODUCTION

24 January — St. Neophytos. Celebrated at the omonimous monastery at Pafos. Neophytos' tomb is decorated with beautiful frescoes. Hundreds of pilgrims flock to the monastery from all over the island.

2 February — The Ypapante of the Chrysoroyiatissa Monastery, not far from Pafos, houses an icon which, according to a local tradition, represents St. Lucas The Apostle.

8 February — St. Theodoros, celebrated at Ktina and at Agios Theodoros.

10 February — St. Charalambos, celebrated at Dhenia, east of Nicosia.

9 March — Forty Martyrs' Day, celebrated at Yiolo, near Pafos.

25 March — Greek National Holiday and the Annunciation; special ceremonies are held at Klirou and Kalavassos.

1 April — Greek Cyprus Day.

6 April — St. Lazaros, patron of Larnaca.

23 April — St. George. Celebrated in many villages; a special ceremony is held at St. George's Monastery in Larnaca.

Good Friday and Easter Sunday (no fixed date).

1 May — Mayday.

50 days after Easter — Harvest festival.

26 July — Agias Paraskevi, celebrated in Nissou, Germasogia and Geroskipou.

15 August — The Dormition of the Virgin Mary, celebrated in all major monasteries: Kykko, Chrysoroyiatissa, Troditissa and Macheras.

14 September — The Exaltation of the Holy Cross, celebrated at the Starrovanni Monastery. On this day hundreds of faithful Christians join in prayer around a fragment of the holy cross, which according to an ancient tradition was brought from the Holy Land by St. Helena.

Last week of September — the Agia Napha festival.

1 October — Independence Day.

18 October — St. Lucas, celebrated in Nicosia, Evrihou, Kolossi and Palekori.

28 October — Greek National Holiday.

21 November — a fair and religious festival in Agros.

25 December — Christmas.

26 December — St. Stephan's Day — second day of Christmas.

How Long to Stay

You will need at least a week to go through the towns and villages, beaches and mountains of Greek Cyprus. But Cyprus is a small island, and even the most conscientious tourist will cover his itinerary in less than two weeks. The Turkish zone, should you reach it, is even smaller. So, read on and then make your own plans!

How Much Will It Cost?

Cyprus' very moderate prices are a good reason to visit. It is cheaper than most of Europe, and even cheaper than some other Middle Eastern countries. Five-star hotels and gourmet restaurants, however, are also expensive in Cyprus. Car rental rates are actually high. Staple foods are very cheap, specially if bought at the marketplace. Public transport, theater, film tickets and other entertainment are also very affordable. Private lodgings are very expensive.

Wandering around Cyprus may be very cheap — a modest couple of hitchhikers will probably manage with less than $50 a day (20 for the night, 20 for food and 5-10 for transportation). Add ten percent for an emergency expense and you will be all right. You will find more information in the following chapters.

The more traditional tourist will opt for 2-3 star hotels ($40 for two), eat at modest restaurants ($25 for two daily — for breakfast and two full meals); transportation will account for $5 — unless they hire a car (about $30).

For the extravagant, $200 a day (for two) will be ample, including the hire of a comfortable car.

What to wear

Having introduced you to the climate, suffice it to stress the need for good walking shoes, for informal sportswear, short-sleeved shirts and a sun-hat in summer, warm woollens and a good parka in winter. Formal dress is required only at the most prestigious hotels. Wear what makes you feel comfortable.

If travelling by boat, bring your own sleeping bag and lots of woollens: at night the deck of a ship will be always very damp and often rather cold, even in the warmer seasons.

*I*NTRODUCTION

Part Three — Easing the Shock: Where are We?

Getting Around

Cyprus is small, and distances are short. The roads, however, are bad: sometimes they shrink to a single lane of broken asphalt, and often, in the mountains, they are little more than a goat track. There is only one highway: from Nicosia to Limassol.

Finding your way around

Street names are clearly indicated in all main towns both in Greek and in English. The original Greek names, however, are freely transliterated into English. This may cause occasional problems: your map mentions, for example "Lidras St."; but all you find at the street corner is "Ledra St". Driving east along the southern coast you reach a sign "Pafos 5 km."; on your map it says "Pafos".

Public Transportation

Buses are by far the most popular and convenient means of transportation. They will get you practically anywhere on the island — but they are rather slow, crowded, stuffy and obsolete. At most Tourist Offices (CTO) you will find a timetable of all major bus lines. Keep it at hand: if you missed your bus, you may have to wait several hours for the next... Buses run from 5.30am to 7pm, but in the high season many lines run until midnight. Prices are surprisingly low.

There is also a **Shared Taxi Service**, more comfortable, faster but also more expensive. Buy your ticket and you will share a taxi with 4-6 other travellers. You may reserve your ticket by telephone, and the taxi will probably pick you up on time at your hotel. This service only runs between the main towns.

Shared taxis are run by the *Kyrdas Inter Express*; you will find further details on the local offices in the itinerary chapters.

There are also, of course, "real" private taxis. They will take you anywhere on the map — for a price. They have a fixed tariff (if you can get hold of it), valid between 6am and 11pm; in the early hours of the morning prices are hitched up by 15%.

Hiring a Car
Following British tradition, motorized vehicles keep to the left side of the road. If you are used to right-side driving, take care.

All the major international agencies (*Eurocar*, *Avis*, *Hertz*...) operate in Cyprus. Their prices are higher than those of local agencies, but their cars are generally more reliable. On the whole, car-hire prices are higher than in Western Europe.

Cars may be hired in one location and returned elsewhere; minimum hire is one full day, and the car has to be returned at the prescribed hour; failure to report on time will result in an additional fee. Most credit cards are accepted.

In the high season, the only way to find a car for hire is by advance reservation through your agent.

In most towns you will also be able to hire motorcycles and bicycles.

Hired vehicles are **not allowed** to cross from the Greek to the Turkish zone.

Private Cars
If you could not bear to leave your car at home, you will be allowed to use it freely during your stay; but if it is a standard model (left-hand drive) you will probably

experience some unease driving on the left side of the street.

As we have already mentioned, road conditions are (except for the only highway) quite rough. Most roads are two way, one or two lanes at most, and the farther you go from urban civilization the higher the risk is of finding yourself travelling along a goat track, indicated as a "country road" on your map. To enjoy your driving in Cyprus, you have to be at least moderately adventurous...

Petrol Stations are commonly found on all main roads; on the highway, keep an eye on your fuel indicator: on the last 25 miles before Limassol there is not a single station!

Petrol stations open for business at 6am and shut at 6pm (Saturdays at 4pm). Some stations remain open throughout the weekend in all towns.

Traffic regulations are standard, except for left-side driving. Children under 5 are forbidden to use the front seat. Distances are indicated in kilometers.

Maximus Speed is 50 Kmh in urban zones, 70 on inter-urban roads and 100 on the highway.

Parking is forbidden along pavements marked with double yellow lines. Single yellow lines allow limited parking, as indicated by sign.

Bicycles
Cyprus is a relatively small island, and most sites are within pedalling reach. Riding a bicycle on Cyprus' roads may however be rather dangerous; in the hilly regions, it is also very exhausting. For further information, call the Cyprus Bicycle-riders Association, Nicosia, 5 Visiinos st., tel. 02-459056. In the itinerary chapters you will find also some programmes suitable for bicycle riders.

Organized Tours
Several agencies offer a wide choice of organized tours. They will take you anywhere (that counts): archaeological

sites, churches and monasteries, quaint villages and nature reserves. Most tours are by bus; others by car, some by boat. There are also some sight-seeing programmes by night.

Regular programmes are morning-to noon or morning-to-night. Overnight tours include a late dinner on site. Boat tours are offered from May to October. Prices are reasonable: around $13 for half-day tours, $20 for full-day tours and night tours; they include picking you up at your hotel, the services of a registered guide and entrance tickets to sites and museums. Children under 12 pay half-price (not in restaurants...). Further details at the CTOs and at most travel agencies.

Accommodation

There are hundreds of hotels, apartment hotels and registered pensions, ranging from luxury 5-star giants to single-starred hovels. There are also unregistered inns and pensions — and youth hostels. The *Cyprus Tourist Organization* (CTO) publishes an almost complete list of hotels, including their classification, rating and services.

At the apartment-hotels you may find studio apartments and 1-3 room suites. Apartment Hotels are relatively cheaper than regular hotels.

Off-season prices are generally 25% lower than summer prices.

In summer it is advisable to reserve rooms in advance, at least in the more fashionable resorts; at your agent's you may also find some interesting bargains, cheaper than what you will find on arrival.

Five-star hotels provide their guests with the utmost luxury in all their services: airconditioning, radio, TV sets, room telephone; swimming pools, bars, restaurants, nightclubs, saunas, tennis courts and other sport facilities. Often they will also offer baby-sitting services, medical care and services for the handicapped.

*I*NTRODUCTION

Four-star hotels provide their guests with high-standard services, similar to their higher-priced competitors.

Three-star hotels are also comfortable and often as good as the higher class resorts.

Two-star hotels are clean and offer good accommodation, but their tourist services are considerably limited and more spartan.

Apartment hotels are classified in two classes — A and B. The services they provide include airconditioned rooms, swimming-pools and a supermarket.

Hotel prices may vary according to class, location and season; average double occupancy rates are as follows:

5-star — $90-150
4-star — $50-90
3-star — $35-50
2-star — $25-35
1-star — $20-25

Apartment hotels:
Class A — $40-60 (room and kitchenette)
Class B — $25-35 (room and kitchenette)

Unclassified hotels are even cheaper.

There are **Youth Hostels** in Nicosia, Pafos, Troodos and Limassol; they cater only to members of the *IYHA* (International Youth Hostel Association). You may buy your IYHA membership at the Nicosia and Limassol Hostels.

Hostel prices range between $4-5 per night, including bedsheets, blankets, service, taxes and breakfast. Showers are generally extra. For further details, apply to *The Cyprus Youth Association*, POB 1328 Nicosia, Cyprus.

Food and Restaurants

There are restaurants on almost every street corner, and in the major resorts, at almost every step. In summer, you will find most of them crowded with tourists. Off season, often the headwaiter will stand at the door, trying to entice you in.

In comparison with European standards, restaurant prices are quite reasonable. Unquestionably, food will not be the highest item on your Cyprus budget.

Unlike their European colleagues, Cypriot restaurateurs offer generally a single menu — take it or leave it. Exotic kitchens are still rare (although you will find several in Nicosia). Greek cuisine is the order of the day — but you probably will not find it difficult to enjoy.

Lunch is generally served 12am-2.30pm; dinner from 7.30pm onward. Restaurant prices are under the control of the CTO (Cyprus Tourism Office); they include a 10% service charge and a 3% CTO tax.

Cypriot cuisine is basically Greek, with some Middle-Eastern nuances, as witnessed by the everpresent *hummous*, *tahina* and *shiskebab*. Lemons are predominant, a true symbol of Greek cuisine.

Your menu will always begin with a *meze* (or *mezedes*, or *mezedakia*). It will appear as a platoon of miniature dishes, with a foretaste of the entire menu. This will include the firsts courses — *hummous* (a chickpeas paste, with paprika and olive oil), *tahina* (a sesame sauce), *zaziki* (cucumbers in yogurth), village salad (tomatoes, cucumbers, olives with olive oil and goat cheese) and home-made *pitas* (flat breads).

For seconds you will have a choice of stuffed vegetables (*dolmades* — the most interesting is undoubtedly the stuffed vine-leaves — *koupepia*); *Haloumi* is smoked pork with a side dish of cheese.

Then come the main servings: *sheftalia* (grilled minced pork), *moussaka* (a slow-baked pie with eggplants, potatoes, minced meat, cheese and lots of spices), *stiffado* (a sort of stew redolent of onion), *afelia* (a pork stew in vine sauce), *tava* (baked lamb with onions) and *shishkebab* — a dish that has already found its place in western menus.

Also very popular are *kleftiko* (baked mutton and potatoes), *fasolada* (baked beans — food of the masses all over the world) and *zalatina* (smoked sausage).

There are, of course, fish restaurants as well, where you will find all sorts of deep sea fish, inkfish, octopus, shrimps and other delicacies.

For those who have a sweet tooth, and are not, at this point, too full to continue, there are several types of oriental sweets, like *souzoukko* (mashed nuts, almonds and other dry fruits in grapes and honey sauce, or *loucoumi* (known in Europe as Turkish Delight) — and a very sweet, very strong and very thick minicup of coffee (if you like it black and unsweeetened, be firm about it!).

If you're on a diet, you may order your own selection from the available menu, but do not be surprised if your bill is higher than that of those who stuffed themselves with the whole *meze*!

Wines
Wine is the pride of all Cyprus' farmers. Their vineyards produce some of the best wines in the world. The hills of Limassol and Pafos and the slopes of the Troodos Mountains are rightly known as some of the best vine-growing lands.

Cyprus' wine was already famous at the time of the de Lusignan (13th and 14th Century). The three main wine-growing regions were (and still are) the Commandaria (near Limassol), Phoenix (near Pafos) and Templar (near Kyrenia). Some of the best Cyprus vines were introduced six centuries ago in the Champagne region (in France). Under the Ottoman rule the wine industry suffered a considerable setback, but as from the end of the 19th Century it has renewed its fame and is still growing.

Today there are four major and very up-to-date wine-cellars (*Etko, Sodap, Loel, Keo*) and some minor, artisan producers. Many are open to visitors, and you will be invited to view the wine-making process and to sample their wines.

Cypriots are not great wine consumers; they prefer brandy, rum and specially *ouzo* (an aniseed liquor).

The most famous of Cyprus' wines is undoubtedly the *Commanderia*. It is made from grapes grown on the Limassol hills. The harvested grapes are left in the open, to bake under the sun, for a fortnight before being processed by hand... and feet. The juice is kept until springtime, when it is brought to the cellars. There it will remain, in special oak barrels and at constant temperature, for ten years.

Keo is a pleasant local beer; the internationally famous *Karlsberg* has a plant in Cyprus too.

Tourist Information
Tourism has been recognized by the government of Cyprus as the major financial resource of the island. The promotion of tourism has become one of the primary goals of the economy. And promotion of tourism means the creation of a wide range of tourist services of the highest possible standards. The CTO (*Cyprus Tourist Organisation*) and its offices offer their assistance for hotel reservations, cultural and entertainment programmes, guided tours, special events, timetables etc. As soon as you reach any town where a CTO desk can be found, you will do well to visit it, asking as many questions as you can think of. Pick up as much written material as you are able to read.

For the Handicapped
The handicapped tourist will find a surprisingly wide network of services in Cyprus, beginning with landing assistance at the airport; special public transportation for wheelchair dependent tourists may be reserved through *Avis* (2 Homer St., POB 2276 Nicosia, tel. 02-472062).

Many hotels are equipped for the provision of services for the handicapped; their list is available at the CTO offices. For further information, apply to *The Pancyprian Organisation for the Disabled*, 50 Pendelis st., Dasoupolis, Nicosia, tel. 02-426301.

*I*NTRODUCTION

Sport
Watersports are very popular in all seaside resorts. Tourists may hire boats, water-skis and diving equipment. at their hotel or at the watersport centres; weather information is available at the Coastal Meteorological Service (tel. 04-652507).

Diving equipment is available at the Divers' Clubs of Pafos, Larnaca, Agia Napa and Limassol (Cyprus Association of Divers, tel. 02-477757). Fishermen will find, a guide to coastal fishing in Cyprus waters, at the Fisheries Dept. of the Ministry of Agriculture, also useful to divers in their underwater encounters with the local population.

Fishing is allowed only in specific reserves, and only to owners of a special permit; information, conditions and restrictions are available to tourists at the CTOs. Underwater fishing is forbidden.

Many hotels are equipped with tennis courts, and usually also offer tennis racquets for hire.

Horse-riding is not a very widespread sport, and is considered a luxury; Nicosia vaunts a riding club, the *Nicosia Riding Club*, POB 1783, Nicosia.

The British Military Bases maintain some good golf courses; a visit as well as a game may be possible.

Soccer is the most popular mass-sport, but its standards lag far behind those of European clubs.

September is the time of the Cyprus International Rally (car races). In winter (January and February), the ski runs of the Troodos are often open to the public. There are two runs for beginners (Sun Valley 1 and 2) and one for professionals (North Face).

Shopping
Compulsive shoppers may find it difficult to satisfy their cravings. Prices are not too high, but the choice is rather poor. Nicosia is the only place that can be rated as an adequate shopping turf.

Shoes and clothes are cheap, but of poor quality.

Woolworth, Marks and Spenser, Benetton and *Stefanel* have local outlets in Nicosia.

Among local crafts, you will find outlets for the famous *Leftaritika* laces, hand-made jewels, silver *Chanapias* (amphors), copper objects, earthenware tools and wickerworks.

General Information

Currency Exchange

Cyprus' currency is the Cypriot pound (CYP), subdivided in 100 cents and worth about $2US.

European currencies and US dollars are welcome everywhere, but you will find it easier to change US dollars, British pounds and German marks. You may be asked to present your passport only when changing banknotes of $100 or travelers' cheques.

Credit Cards — *Master Card, Visa, Eurocard* etc. — are quickly taking their rightful place throughout Cyprus, specially in Nicosia and at the seaside resorts. Banknotes or travelers' cheques, however, are more welcome.

Banks are open Monday-Saturday, 8.30-12.30am; in the afternoon you may change money at the Tourist Centres (3-5.30pm in winter and 4-6.30pm in summer). The airport money-changers at Larnaca and Pafos are open around-the-clock, even on Sunday; money-changers stay open very late also at the seaports.

Do not change all your money on arrival — but make sure you have enough local currency to last you over the weekend.

Working Hours

Most shops open their doors for business at 8am, closing for a siesta at 1-4pm, and end their day at 9pm. In winter their siesta is shortened to 2.30pm, and close at 5.30pm.

Wednesday and Saturday afternoons most shops are closed.

Public services run a five-day week, 7.30am-2.30pm (in winter only until 2pm) and stay closed Saturday and Sunday.

Other offices open 8am-1pm and 4-7pm (in winter 2.30-5.30pm) and keep a five day week (closure on Saturday and Sunday).

Petrol stations are open 6am-6pm (Saturday only until 4pm); most of them do not open on Sunday.

Consular services are open Monday to Friday, 9.30-12.30am.

Posts and Telephones
In every town you will find at least one post office, open 8am-1pm; Central post offices also open at 3.30-5.30pm. International trunk calls can be made directly from the Telephone Office and from many public phones; the international call prefix is 00, followed by the code of the target country.

Local calls via public phones cost 2 cents; interurban calls cost 10-20 cents. You will find many public phones equipped for the use of a *Telecard*; telecards are on sale at the post offices and at several kiosks for CYP 2, 5 and 10.

The area codes are:

Nicosia 02; Larnaca 04; Limassol 05; Pafos and Polis 06; Paralimni and Agia Napa 03.

The Media
The *CBC* net (FM, 94.8) broadcasts news in several foreign languages (English, German, French, Swedish and Arabic). The British military transmitter *BFBS* broadcasts in FM (89.4 for Nicosia and 99.6 for Larnaca). The *BBC* overseas programs and the *VOA* (Voice of America) are also available to English speaking listeners.

The local press is, of course, mainly in Greek. There are one English language daily — the *Cyprus Mail* — and two weeklies, the *Cyprus Weekly* and the *Middle East Economic Survey.*

Films and Theatres
Cinemas open daily at 7.30pm; during weekends they screen three daily shows: 3.30pm, 7.30pm and 9.45pm. Foreign films often have English subtitles, Greek films are never translated.

Tips
Tips are always welcome. As for the size of the tip, there are no clear norms. Bills generally include a 10% service charge; perhaps the best policy is to leave the small change for a tip,. Waiters, drivers, barbers and porters do expect to be tipped. The normal porter tip is 50 cents per item — in 5-star hotels at least 1CYP.

Health
In all Cyprus hospitals and major clinics doctors generally speak at least one European language.

The clinics open at 9am and close at 7pm, with a lunch break 1-3pm. Tourists with valid insurance policies can be reimbursed.

Chemist's keep to the regular trade timetable. The address of emergency chemists, which remain open around-the-clock, is available at tel. 192 or, in Nicosia only, tel. 462118.

During summer, beware of too much sun; sun-lotions are necessary for your skin protection — and they are on sale at every supermarket, perfumery and chemist's.

It is better to avoid drinking tap water; bottled mineral water is available everywhere.

It goes without saying that you should always carry a small first aid kit, with a few plasters and your favourite pain-killers.

Chronically ill and allergy-prone tourists will of course bring their medications with them. If you wear glasses, bring an extra pair, just in case.

Personal Security
Cyprus is a law-abiding country, with little if any violence in the streets, at any hour of the day and night. Even young women walking alone are seldom molested. Probably the highest risk one incurs on the street is — the sun.

If you drive, be careful. Cyprus roads are barely adequate, and left side driving may be a hazard, not only if you are a regular right-side driver, but also if — as is often the case — the driver you pass is a right-side driver.

Weights and Measures
Cyprus has recently joined the metric system, but old customs are hard to die:

1 *pic* - 61 cm.
1 *yard* - 91.44 cm.
1 *oke* - 1.28 kg.
1 *gallon* - 4.54 l.

Electric current is, like everywhere else in Europe, 220V; however, do not forget to check on the spot.

Local time is GMT +2.

Visiting Cyprus — Step by Step
This book aims to provide the reader with a practical guide to the highlights of Cyprus. Our itineraries cover the entire island, in an easy-to-follow geographical sequence.

Your starting point will probably be Larnaca or Pafos (the only two international airports on the island), or, coming by sea, Limassol. Visitors to the Turkish side will arrive at Kyrenia or Ercan (a small airport near Nicosia).

We will start out with Larnaca the first step most

visitors take, from here we will proceed to Limassol, following the coastline to Pafos. We shall then cross the **Troodos Mountains** to reach Nicosia. From here visitors may cross over to the Turkish zone, or turn to the coastal plain.

How long it will take? That depends on your itinerary and your stamina: you may carry on, step by step, to the very end, or you may pause wherever you wish — on the mountains, or at one of the alluring beaches of Cyprus, or at some lonely old monastery.

For those who wish to cross over to the Turkish zone, we have added a brief chapter along the northern shores of the island, as well as a sketch of Turkish Nicosia (see the "Nicosia" chapter.

*I*NTRODUCTION

CYPRUS

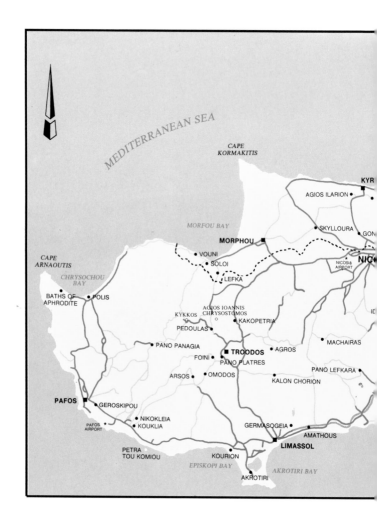

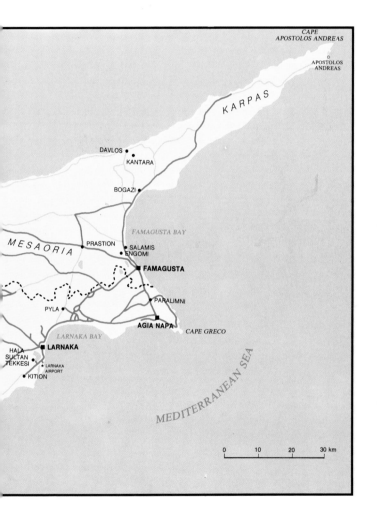

CYPRUS

Larnaca

Larnaca, the most modern of Cyprus' towns, is situated on the Nicosia-Limassol highway, and is just an hours' drive away from both Nicosia and Limassol. Larnaca owes much of its glamour to its airport, which since the closure of its former competitor at Nicosia, is the only international airport on the island. A few miles eastward, at Dhekelia, are some of the most attractive beaches in the Eastern Mediterranean, as well as dozens of modern luxury and apartment hotels. Larnaca itself has a population of 50,000 people.

Larnaca's former name was Kition or Kittim (one of Noah's descendents). The name Larnaca is derived from the Greek word *larnax* (coffin), probably a reminder of the many ancient coffins found on Kition's grounds.

Kition was one of the towns settled by the Mycaeneans in the 13th Century BC, which makes it the most ancient town in Cyprus. Under the Ottoman and the British rule, Larnaca was the main trade centre of the island. At the beginning of our century it lost its rank, first to Famagusta (1918) and later to Limassol. Its seaport today seldom sees large ships — but it still caters to hundreds of private yachts. It has several industrial plants, as well as a large oil refinery. Now, with Famagusta in the Turkish zone, Larnaca is slowly rebuilding its overseas trade.

How to get there
By Air: The airport is situated less than 2 miles from the town centre. It is the National Tender *Cyprus Airways* base and is also used by foreign airlines landing in Cyprus as well as by many charter flights. A taxi service connects the airport with the centre of town; a bus line — No. 21 — also commutes from town to airport — on average only once an hour but very cheap. The last bus leaves

Larnaca — the marina

at 5.30pm in winter, at 7pm in summer, and at 1pm on Saturday. There is no bus service on Sundays.

By Sea: Shipping lines do not use the port of Larnaca, apart from an occasional cruise-boat. The yacht Marina, on the other side is one of the largest and most frequented by European and Middle Eastern yachtsmen.

Larnaca may also be reached by *water-taxi* from Agia Napa. The crossing takes an hour and costs CYP 2.50; it sails from Agia Napa's fishermen's pier to the Larnaca Marina. A timetable is available at George's, on the Marina (tel. 04-624118).

By Land: Its bus terminal extends along the whole length of Leoforos Athinon Ave., the main promenade of the town, alongside the Marina. It serves as a terminal for the Nicosia, Limassol, Pafos, Agia Napa and Troodos bus lines. The airport bus stops in front of the *Sun Hall* Hotel. The *Kellenos* Company buses leave for Nicosia once an hour from 5.45am to 4.45pm, and for Limassol every two hours, also from 5.45am to 4.45pm. Don't expect Swiss precision, however!

The seaside promenade at Larnaca

The *EMAN* Company handles the Agia Napa line, with hourly buses in summer (every two hours in winter).

Shared taxis coming from Nicosia and Limassol stop at Sileos Paveou St., not far from the Marina.

Tourist Services

Larnaca's CTO (Cyprus Tourist Organisation) is situated at the Marina entrance, at the northern end of Athinon Ave. (tel. 654322). Here you will find a map of Larnaca, various information material and a timetable of the urban bus network. Another CTO office located at the airport is open around-the-clock. At the airport you will also find around-the-clock bank services and a flight information desk. The CTO will assist you with hotel reservations and guided tour programmes. Cyprus Airways also has an office at the airport.

All major Cyprus banks have branches in Larnaca. You will find most of them on Zinons Kitieos St. (the main shopping centre) and further north, on Makarios Ave. The

Bank of Cyprus, a few steps past the corner of Zinonos Kitieos and Sileos Pavlou, is open to tourists also in the afternoon.

Larnaca's post office is also located on Zinonos Kitieos, north of the Sileos Pavlou corner.

The Telephone Office is on Lordou Vyronos St., also not far from the shopping centre.

Car Hire
Most car-hire agencies have branches in Larnaca. Some local firms have their only base in Larnaca. At the airport you will find *Hertz, Avis, Europcar* and the large local firm of *A. Petsas*. All four also have downtown branches:

Europcar: Artemidos Ave., 7-8 Joanna Court, tel. 657442, 657462.
Hertz: 33F Leoforos Makariou, tel. 655145; at the airport, tel. 622388.
A. Petsas: Gr. Afxentiou Ave., Carithers ct., tel. 623033; at the airport, tel. 657850.
Avis: 43 Makarios Ave., tel. 657132; at the airport, tel. 657920.

Accommodation
There is a wide choice of hotels and apartment hotels. The downtown hotels are suitable for shorter stays, and are also somewhat cheaper. The hotels on the north-eastern beach strip are of the sea resort type, well equipped with entertainment and sport facilities and medical assistance; they are generally very up-to-date and rather more expensive.

5-Star
Golden Bay: Larnaca-Dhekelia Rd., tel. 04-623444. Far from the town centre, along the coastal road to Agia Napa. A true luxury resort, with a wide selection of services: TV in all rooms, facilities for the handicapped, conference halls, sauna, tennis courts, shopping arcade etc.

4-Star
Palm Beach: Larnaca Dhekelia Rd., tel. 04-657500. Larnaca's best 4-star hotel, with 5-star services (room

TV is an extra!); no services for the handicapped. Also on the beach strip.

Sandy Beach: Larnaca Dhekelia Rd., tel. 04-624333. On the same strip.

Sun Hall: Athinon Ave., tel. 04-653341. Very central; no private beach.

3-Star

Beau Rivage: Larnaca Dhekelia Rd., tel. 04-623600. On the strip, with private beach.

Flamingo Beach: Pyiale Pasa, tel. 04-621621. South of the town centre; no private beach; nice swimming pool; reasonably priced.

Four Lanterns: 19 Athinon Ave., tel. 04-652011. Central; no beach and no pool.

2-Star

Arion: 26 Galileo St., tel. 04-621200. Conveniently located, close to the centre of town and the shopping centre. Swimming pool.

Les Palmiers Sun Hotel: on the corner of Athinon ave. and Pieridou st., tel. 04-627200. Air-conditioned rooms; no beach and no pool.

Eva: Larnaca Dhekelia Rd., tel. 04-624100. On the north-eastern strip; some air-conditioned rooms; swimming pool.

I.B. Sandbeach Hotel: Piyale Pesa, tel. 04-655437. Pleasant beach; no air-conditioning. On the southern strip.

Inexpensive Hotels

Pavion: 11 St. Lazarus Sq., tel. 04-656688. Central, with some air-conditioned rooms. Open only during the high season: better inquire!

The Rainbow Hill: 140 Zinons Kitieos, tel. 04-655874. Near St. Lazaros Sq.; simple and cheap.

Apartment Hotels

Corinthia Beach: Larnaca Dhekelia Rd., tel. 04-624037. A Class. On the beach strip. Swimming pool, studio apartments, one and two-room suites.

Sunflower: 69 Leoforos Makariou, tel. 04-621111. A Class. No beach, no pool, on the Larnaca-Agia Napa road. Studio apartments and 1-2 room suites.

Acropolis: corner of Ermou St. and Grigori Afxentiou Ave.,

LARNACA

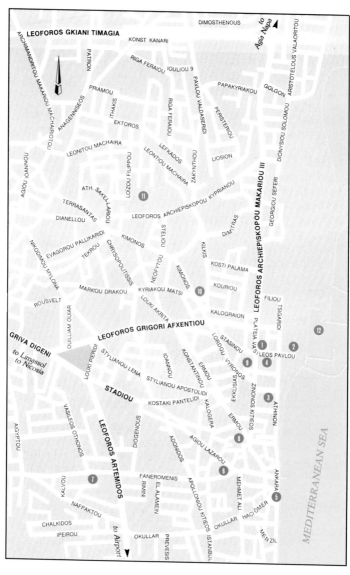

Index

1. CTO office
2. *E.M.A.N.* Terminal
3. *Lefkaritis* Terminal
4. *Makris* Taxi Service
5. Larnaca Castle
6. Agiou Lazarou Church
7. Agia Faneromeni Church
8. Larnaca Market
9. Pierides Museum
10. Larnaca Archaeological Museum
11. Ancient Kition's Acropolis
12. Marina

CYPRUS

Kition

tel. 04-623700. B Class, central; studio apts. and 1-3 room suites; air-conditioned; swimming pool.
Athene Beach: 80 Athinon Ave., on the mall, tel. 04-656272. B Class, central; studio apts. and 1-2 room suites; air-conditioned.
Adonis Beach: Piyale Pasa, tel. 04-656644. B Class, far south of the town; no beach, no pool; air-conditioned.
Boronia: Larnaca-Dhekelia Rd., tel. 04-624200. On the eastern strip; swimming pool; only one-room suites.

Camping
The Camping site is 5 miles east of Larnaca, on the beach, in an eucalyptus grove, on the way to Agia Napa. Showers, toilets, minimarket and restaurant; tents for hire; electrical sockets.

Restaurants
Along the Athinou Ave. shopping arcade you will find dozens of restaurants, fixed menus and prices; no need to reserve tables.

On the Larnaca-Agia Napa Road, along Palm Beach, you will find the *Yin Yang* Chinese restaurant.

Megalos Pefkos is a seafood restaurant, situated at the foot of the castle, on the beach.

Clunis, on Watkins St., tel. 04-128060, is a highly recommended international restaurant.

Mac's, 30 Makariou Ave., is a convenient, inexpensive fast-food spot.

Cafe Retro, 7 Afxentiou Ave., is a pleasant downtown snack-bar and coffee house.

Shopping
The main shopping areas are Hermes, Zinonos Kitieos and Grigoris Afxentiou — three very narrow streets, with lots of large modern shops and traditional boutiques; no department stores. Mostly clothes and footwear, less home appliances and electronics.

Transportation
The streets are not too crowded, and are pleasant to drive along in a car or bike; however, there are few parking facilites. The buses are cheap but outdated; and, of course, there are many private taxis.

What to see
Familiarize yourself with the town map, remembering a few key points: the beach strip, from Athinon Ave. southward along Ankara St. and Piyale Pasa. At the northern end of this promenade, you will find the Marina. Parallel to the beach runs the Zinonos Kitieos shopping arcade, extending northward on Leoforos Makariou III, toward the Agia Napa Road. Lordou Vyronos (Lord Byron) St. and Kimonos St., branch off from Zinonos Kitieos towards ancient Kition and the suburbs.

Our itinerary begins at **Larnaca Castle**, on Ankara St., along the beach. The castle was built in 1625 and originally served as a prison. From its promenade walls, you will enjoy a view of the Scala Quarter with its Büyük Kebir Mosque — formerly one of Larnaca's Turkish neighbourhoods. Today the castle houses an archaeological museum, dedicated to ancient Kition and to later periods (open Monday-Friday, 7.30am-1.30pm, tel. 04-630169); entrance fee.

From the castle, continue north along Ankara St. and turn left on Dionysus. After a short walk you will reach the Faneromenis-Agios Lazarou corner, where you will see the **Agiou Lazarou Church**, built in the 9th century by Emperor Leo, on the site of St. Lazaros' tomb, in honour of the town's Patron Saint. According to legend, after his resurrection, Lazaros traveled to Larnaca and became its first bishop. His tomb is inside the church, under the main altar. The entrance is decorated with a number of icons; one of them depicts Lazaros' resurrection. The church belltower was built in 1857.

Not far from that corner, along Leoforos Faneromenis, is the **Agia Faneromeni Church**, built in the 8th century above an ancient cave.

Return to St. Lazaros Church, and turn left along Ermou St. After a short walk, you will find yourself at the **Larnaca Market**, with Zinonos Kitieos St. on your right. This is one of the main shopping areas of Larnaca. Walk along it, enjoying the colourful shop-windows.

Beyond Lordou Vyronos St. (more about it later on), stands the **Pierides Museum**, with an imposing private archaeological collection, founded 1840 and later donated to the City. The museum is open Monday-Friday, 9am-1pm; entrance fee.

Proceed now on Lordou Vyronos St., and follow it north-westward to where it crosses Grigori Afxentiou Ave. and becomes Kimonos St. About 200 yards further on you will find the **Larnaca Archaeological Museum**, on the grounds of the Sisters' School of St. Joseph's (1844). In the museum several Neolithic and Bronze Age objects are exhibited, recovered in local digs. Open June-August, Monday-Saturday, 7.30am-1.30pm — and the rest of the year Monday-Friday, 7.30am-2pm; Saturdys only until 1pm. Entrance fee.

About 300 yards past Kimonos, you will reach **Ancient Kition's Acropolis**, one of Cyprus' ancient towns, which was for a time the capital of the whole island. Little

Hala Sultan Tekke Mosque

remains of the ancient city, once rich with temples and palaces: a few remnants of Heracles' and Aphrodite's temples — and the site where recent digs uncovered several gold, bronze and ivory tombs of the 13th century BC.

Proceed to Archiepiskopou Kyprianou Ave.; at the corner you will see the 19th century Krissopolitissa Church. Turn right, to the **Kition Archaeologic Site**. Recent archaeological digs have proved that Kition was founded by Mycenean traders in the 13th century BC, destroyed toward the end of that century and rebuilt by a new wave of Aegean immigrants. The Phoenicians conquered the town in the late 9th century BC, and from here tried to invade the inland. The Phoenicians held the town for three centuries, only to surrender it to Ptolomeus I of Syria. The site is open Monday-Saturday, 7.30am-2pm; on winter Saturdays only until 1pm. Entrance fee.

This is the most important of four recently opened archaeological sites, with no less than five temples of the

13th and 12th century BC and traces of a number of other structures. The first walls of Kition, made of enormous boulders, date from that period.

Continue now along Kilkis St., and turn left on Makarios Ave. From there, turn right into Sileos Pavlou St. and to the **Marina**, where you will also find the CTO office.

We will end our Larnaca itinerary with a leisurely walk southward, along the seaside promenade, with its quaint but attractive restaurants and bars.

Several small yachts, and other boats offering coastal tours as far as Famagusta, are moored at the Marina Pier. For detailed information, call Captain George, tel. 638505, 624118.

The Salt Lake

Leave town along the airport access road and you'll soon come across the **Larnaca Salt Lake**. This lake, which in winter is full and frequented by flights of flamingoes, dries up by the end of July and its bed grows a 2-3 inch thick crust of salt. Apparently the lake was once connected to the sea, but was artificially transformed into a salt-water basin, to be duly harvested in the late summer months.

According to a legend, the salt lake was formed when a local woman refused Lazarus a bunch of grapes from her vineyard; the affronted Saint cursed the offender, changing her vineyard into a barren salt lake...

The truth is, of course, quite less dramatic. The area used to be a shallow, and particularly salty lagoon, which dried up in summer. Its salt was harvested since ancient times, and later on, its mouth was artificially closed and the lagoon became a "lake". Salt in those times was a mineral so precious, that the Roman soldiers' wages were often paid in salt: in fact the term *salary* derives from the latin word *salis* (salt).

Between the 12th and 14th centuries AD. Larnaca was a very important seaport, and salt was its main commodity. Salt harvesting is run by the State, but only for local use.

The harvest is done in part manually and in part by

specially equipped small tractors. The salt is carried to trucks for transportation to the packing plants.

The Hala Sultan Tekke Mosque

This Moslem shrine is located on the western shore of the Salt Lake. It was built in 1816, on the site of Umm Haram's Tomb. According to tradition, she was Mohammed's foster mother, and died here of a broken neck, falling from her donkey, during one of the Moslim raids in 647. The Mosque is open to visitors June-September, 7.30am-7.30pm (in winter only until sunset). Entrance free.

The Angeloktistos Church

On the same road, about 7 miles from Larnaca, is the village of Kiti (or Kition), with the **Panagia Angeloktistos**, an imposing 11th century Byzantine structure, with a later (14th century) Gothic front. Its floors contain a 6th century mosaic, depicting the Virgin Mary with the infant in her arms, and the Archangels Michael and Gabriel at her sides; on the walls are several icons from various periods.

Pyla

Leave Larnaca via Agia Napa. Little more than four miles out of Larnaca, along the gulf, not far from the *Palm Beach Hotel*, turn left and proceed about one mile, to the village of **Pyla**.

Until 1974 this was a mixed Greek-Turkish settlement. Pyla is located within the territory of Greek Cyprus. It stands on the area of the British Dhekelia Base, and has become a joint Turkish-Greek enclave, policed by a United Nations contingent.

Pyla's church and its belltower date from the Middle Ages.

The Beaches

The Larnaca Turist beach is administered by the CTO. It is a 6 mile strip running toward Agia Napa, and is equipped with dressing rooms, showers, beach-chairs, snack-bars and restaurants.

Night Spots

Larnaca's night-life is not too hectic. "Late" (8-9pm) hour entertainment is limited to a leisurely walk along the promenade, or sitting at one of the promenade's many cafés and restaurants.

Disco fans will be able to dance at the *Laser Disco* (in Makarios Ave., north of downtown, near the *Sunflower* apartment hotel — or at *Spilia Disco*, on Lordou Vyronos St.

There are also a few Greek music spots: the *Phantasia Night Club*, *Dolce Vita* and *Nostalgia*, all of them on General Timagia St., near the Makarios Ave. corner.

At the Marina entrance you will find the *Marina Pub.*

Sport

The *Larnaca Tennis Club* — with its six tennis courts — is at 10 Kilkis St., tel. 656999.

At the Tourist Beach of Larnaca you will find watersport facilities, and the *Louis Loizou Diving Centre* (33 Evanthis Pierides St., tel. 04-627091).

Useful Addresses and Telephone Numbers

Larnaca prefix: 04.
First Aid, Police, Fire Brigade: tel. 199.
Hospital: tel. 652265.
Flight Information: tel. 654389 (around-the-clock).
Cyprus Airways: tel. 623036.
Hotel reservations: tel. 654486.
Airport Bank (around-the-clock): tel. 652848, 654330.
CTO at Democratias Sq., tel. 654322.

Agia Napa

Agia Napa is known as a famous tourist resort throughout Europe. It is one of Cyprus' most popular resorts, especially among German and Scandinavian tourists.

This little village has less than 1000 inhabitants, but

AGIA NAPA

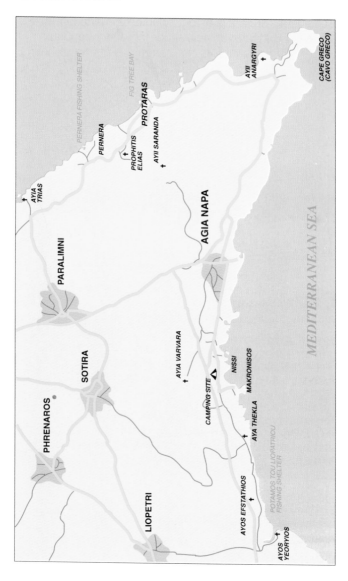

thanks to its unique location and splendid beaches, it hosts 10-15 thousand tourists daily, during the summer season! The beaches are strips of soft and thin sand, hidden among a chain of rocky boulders, which form many small and cosy bays. In summer the entire population of Agia Napa turns into tourist-caterers, working at hotels, restaurants, supermarkets, discos, car-hire and bicycle agencies. There are also lots of gift-shops and other tourist-traps; footwear, clothes and whatever one may need to buy.

The village owes its name, according to tradition, to a hunting party that, wandering in the forest, found an ancient cave, with a splendid icon inside it. Hence from "Napa" (= forest) and "Agia" (= saint) — Agia Napa (= The Forest Lady-Saint).

The main centre of the district is Paralimni, 3 miles north of Agia Napa itself. East of the village is Protaras, now also becoming a tourist resort.

How to get there
By Bus: there is an hourly minibus service that connects regularly (on the hour) Larnaca and Agia Napa, from the *Sun Hall Hotel* in Larnaca to the CTO Office in Agia Napa and vice versa. There is also a sporadic taxi service (9b Velouchiotis St., tel. 03-722440), and, of course, one may order a private taxi (CYP 7.50 per ride).

Those coming from elsewhere on the island will have to stop over in Larnaca; in the summer, however, there is a daily direct bus, leaving Nicosia (at Solomos Sq.) in the morning and returning in the late afternoon (inquire at tel. 02-473414).

By sea: *Water Taxi* from the Larnaca Marina (tel. 04-624118).

Tourist Services
The CTO Office (tel. 03-721796) is very central, in front of the Monastery. Here you will find information on the district's hotels and beaches, in Agia Napa, Paralimni and Protaras — and good maps of the whole district. The CTO

will also assist you, with hotel reservations (in summer, however, you should book your rooms in advance).

Almost all the major car-hire agencies are represented in Agia Napa:

A. Petsas: halfway between the monastery and the *Grecian Bay Hotel*, tel. 03-721260.
Avis: right in centre, tel. 03-721844.
Europcar: halfway to the fishermen's pier, tel. 03-721031.
Hertz: Misiauli Kavazoglou St., tel. 03-721836.
Budget is represented by *A. Petsas*.

All sorts of motorcycles and bicycles are available for hire at scores of local agencies.

The village has branches of several banks, most of them are open for money-changing in the afternoon as well.

The post office is near the monastery. To reach it, walk north, and turn right after the *Bank of Cyprus* branch.

Accommodation
For the high season it is important to book rooms ahead of your visit. It is best to make your reservation through your local agent, who will provide ample information on the district's hotels. Should you find yourself in Agia Napa without accommodation, apply to the local CTO; they will try to help you, but in full season even they may fail. Your only hope will be to try some hotel desk.

At the Grecian Beach, the Sandy Beach and the Nissi Beach you will find clusters of hotels and apartment hotels. In Protaras and Paralimni there are also several hotels and apartment hotels.

5-Star
Grecian Bay Hotel: little more than half a mile from the village, with its own private beach (tel. 03-721301). The peak of local luxury — and, on season, the peak of Cyprus prices. Swimming pools, tennis courts, disco, sauna, *Bank of Cyprus* branch. Anything you need without leaving its grounds.

4-Star
Grecian Sands: a little beyond the *Grecian Bay*, on the

way to Protaras (tel. 721616). Private beach and pools, tennis courts, disco; not less attractive, while substantially cheaper than the *Grecian Bay*.

Nissi Beach: About 1.5 mile west of Agia Napa (tel. 03-721021). A little too far from the village's hectic night life, but it has everything that counts: beach, pool, tennis, sauna and diving club.
Florida: Between the *Grecian Bay* and the *Grecian Sand*, but across the road (tel. 03-721821). Very reasonable prices, but no private beach. A small hotel, with a small pool, tennis courts and sauna.

3-Star
Bella Napa Bay: tel. 03-721601. East of the village; no private beach, but with a pleasant swimming pool and good tennis courts.
Napa Mermaid: near the *Bella Napa Bay*, same standards of prices and services, but no tennis courts. Tel. 03-721606.
Nissi Park: Near the omonimous beach. Tel. 03-721121; pool, no private beach; room phone and TV.
Sunwing: Kryou Nerou Ave., tel. 03-721806. The only 3-star hotel with a private beach, and this is reflected in the prices. Less than one mile east of the village. It also has a swimming pool and tennis courts.

Inexpensive hotels
1 and 2-star hotels are less comfortable; the following, however, may be pleasant for a short stay:

Chrysland: 2-star, tel. 03-721311. West of the village, no beach.
Leros: 1-star, tel. 03-721126. Very close to the village, on the road to the fishermen's pier.

Apartment Hotels
Those willing to do without the luxuries of hotel lobbies, room and restaurant service, twice daily change of bedclothes and towels, can save money by staying at one of the resort's apartment hotels. The rooms are spacious and pleasant, and most of them are modern, conveniently located and equipped with swimming pools.

Agia Napa — the monastery

A Class

Anesis: Modern, close to the village and to the Golden Sands Beach; tel. 03-721104. 1-2 room suites, with modern kitchens and a pleasant sitting room. A small pool, snack-bar, bar, and a TV room.

Anthea: A stone throw south of the monastery, on the road to Larnaca; tel. 03-721411. Two floors, with 84 suites with sitting room, bedroom, terrace, kitchen and showers; heated and air-conditioned; snackbar, restaurant, pool and supermarket.

Limanaki Beach: tel. 03-721600. At the fishermen's pier, south of the village, very close to the Golden Sands Beach. Studios and 1 room suites, with terrace, kitchen, sitting area, toilets and bathroom or shower. Snackbar, pool and TV room. Air-conditioned.

All three are conveniently priced. Others are slightly cheaper. A Class apartment hotels, can be found further away, west of the village (*Nissiana*, tel. 03-721224, not far from the Nissi Beach) or eastward (*Kermia Beach*, tel. 03-721401).

B Class

Adams Beach: tel. 03-721275, on the Nissi Beach, 1.5 mile from the village. Excellent range of services: private beach, pool and tennis courts.

Antia Maria: tel. 03-721921. Central, near the CTO. Inexpensive, but no pool. Very close to the beach.

Castalia: tel. 03-721108, on the west side of the village. Restaurant, supermarket, shopping arcade. With 78 1-3 room suites, all air-conditioned and fully equipped. At walking distance from the Sandy Beach. Swimming pool, restaurant and TV room. Next door to a bicycle and motorbike hiring agency.

Freminore: tel. 03-721711, near the *Castalia*; same services and prices. Small swimming pool; next door to supermarket.

Cornelia: tel. 03-721406; near the CTO. Small, inexpensive, but no pool; 1-2 room suites.

Eleana: tel. 03-721640. Just opened, half way between the village and the Golden Sands Beach. One room suites only, with a bed corner in the sitting room. Fully equipped, air-conditioned, bar, snackbar, pool, TV room and minimarket.

Camping
The only camping grounds in Agia Napa are situated west of the village, near the beach (tel. 03-721946). Showers, toilets, minimarket, bar, tents for hire and electrical sockets. Open from March to October.

Restaurants
Along the two main streets of the village — Leoforos Makariou and Agias Mavris — there are scores of restaurants serving local cuisine all similarly priced. The monastery side is crowded, but the upper end of Agias Mavris is quiet and attractive. *Kantara*, at the Ritsou Yianni corner, is recommended.

Cyprus House (1 Hilovris St.), has a *bouzouki* band.
Lourenzos, also very central (tel. 03-771686), has a *meze* and steak house.

Nightlife
This is mainly a youthful resort, and the night life is obviously louder and longer than anywhere else in Cyprus. The *Majestic* discoteque is located within the *Karousos* apartment hotel, at the western end of the village; *VIP* is a restaurant with disco, across the street from the CTO office.

Diving
Sun Fish Diving Centre: 26 Makarios Ave., tel. 03-721300.
Flying Fish Diving Centre: *Nissi Beach* hotel, tel. 03-721021.
Trum Diving Centre: *Capo Bay* hotel, Paralimni, tel. 03-131101.

Beaches
The Agia Napa district has the best beaches on the island. The **Ayia Thekla** Beach is situated 4 miles west of the village; it is a small, relatively isolated beach. The **Makronisos** Beach is much closer to the village — less than one mile away — it has three small and pleasant

sand coves. The **Nissi** Beach, 2 miles west of the village, is sheltered by the Nissi islot; it is a hotel and restaurant cluster, with a wide range of seaside services. The **Sandy Beach** is also very well sheltered and equipped.

The main, and most crowded Agia Napa Beach is **Golden Sands**, east of the fishermen's pier. It is also, of course, very well serviced.

A walk along the beaches, on a beautiful day, may be very pleasant indeed. Start from the village towards Sandy Beach; visit the **Agios Georgios Church**, then turn westward to the beaches; enjoy the scenery and the bikinis.

Protaras, less than 6 miles from Agia Napa, also has two excellent beaches: **Flamingo Bay** and **Fig Tree Bay**.

Shopping
Agia Napa is only a small village, but it has some very good shops, to be found along Makariou, Kryou Nerou and Eleftherias Sts. Many gift shops, footwear, clothing and electronics.

What to see
The only historical site is the **monastery** — one of the last palaces built by the Venetians before they lost the island in 1570. On the monastery grounds was a cave, where according to tradition, some hunters found the icon that gave the village its name.

The entrance gate and gatehouse are characteristic of Venetian architecture. The monastery's water supply is provideded by a Roman style aqueduct, ending in two cysterns. In the inner court you will see a curious pig-shaped water-fountain.

The monastery was built to serve the local Catholic community. Later it was impounded by the Greek-Orthodox Church. In 1974 it became a shelter for displaced Greek refugees fleeing from the Turkish sector, and specially from Famagusta. A new wing was added in 1978, and it serves as a hostel and a multi-faith religious centre.

Toward the end of September the monastery hosts an annual three-day festival, with art exhibitions, entertainment and various shows.

The Agia Napa District
Protaras and Paralimni
A visit to Protaras and Paralimni is a must. It is a very pleasant 20 mile itinerary for cycles (motored or not).

Start toward the south-eastern end of the island, **Cape Greco**. Near the promontory, where the roads snakes northward, turn right onto a narrow lane climbing to the promontory itself, with its impressive boulders and ridges. Back to the main road, proceed northward for about 3 miles to Protaras, a small village now quickly becoming a tourist resort.

Follow the road northward; turn right to visit the **Agios Trias Church**, high on the beach. The road proceeds to the border with the Turkish Zone, 2 miles further on, towards Famagusta. Turn left to Paralimni.

Paralimni
Paralimni is the largest centre in the district. Its CTO is open from July to September. The Paralimni Church is **Agios Georgiou**.

From Paralimni you will turn back southward to Agia Napa.

A Walk to Paralimni
A 9 mile walk will take you to Cape Greco and to Protaras. If one gets too tired, the buses can always be reached and stopped from the roadside.

Start from Agia Napa along the main road to Protaras. After less than a mile, where the road turns northward near the *Sunwing* hotel, leave the road and follow the path that runs along sand beaches and rocky boulders toward Cape Greco. Don't walk barefoot!

Approaching the Cape, you will see a small lighthouse and the towering aerials used by Radio Monte Carlo. The promontory itself (with the lighthouse and the aerials)

Stavrovouni Monastery

cannot be reached; but the wild beauty of its majestic boulders will leave you breathless. From the locked gate you may reach the access road and finally the Agia Napa-Protaras road, to return by taxi or by bus.

Should you wish to carry on to Paralimni (4 additional miles), turn right on the Agia Napa-Protaras road, and after a few hundred yards turn right again toward the **Agia Anargyri Church**. Follow the winding path for less than half a mile, turn left and carry on along the rocky shore to Protaras. You will enjoy the sight of Cape Greco, then you will come across an ancient cave, an old windmill and finally Protaras itself, one of Cyprus' gems and one of its major future resorts.

Return to Agia Napa by taxi or by bus.

From Larnaca to Limassol
The forty-odd miles that separate Larnaca from Limassol are not too interesting. First you will travel on a crowded and narrow asphalt motorway (a slow and rather enervating drive); after about 20 miles the sideroad

reaches the Nicosia-Limassol highway, and the driver may relax.

The Stavrovouni Monastery stands on top of a 2000 feet mount, towering above its rather flat reaches. It is the most ancient monastery in Cyprus, built by St. Helena in the year 330. Among the most treasured relics preserved in the Monastery is a fragment of "The True Cross", brought over from the Holy Land by the founding Saint (mother of Emperor Constantine). Today the monastery houses about a dozen monks.

The monastery is less than 30 miles from Larnaca. Leave town westward on the Limassol highway, and after 3 miles, at the road junction, turn right toward Kalon Chorion, proceeding to Agia Anna and to the old Nicosia-Limassol road. Here turn left, and the lane will take you to the monastery. If possible do it on a Sunday: on weekdays the site is closed to visitors.

If the weather is good and you feel like a pleasant two-hour walk, leave your car at the Spithoudia sign, on the access road to the monastery. Turn left and follow the path beyond the water-pump. The path climbs the hillside to the top — and to the monastery.

Not far from the Spithoudia sign you will see a second, smaller monastery — **Agia Varvara**.

Lefkara
15 miles out of Larnaca on the same road, you will come to Kofinou. Past this village you will come to a turnoff to the right, toward Lefkara.

It is a taxing road, winding through the hills for about 6 miles toward **Pano Lefkara** and **Kato Lefkara** (Upper and Lower Lefkara). Two exquisite mountain hamlets. The tourist centre is in Pano Lefkara.

Lefkara is famous for its lace — the *Lefkaritika* lace. You will find it on sale at scores of shops, together with the usual silver and copper objects and other tourist wares. You will find the lace very expensive indeed.

According to a legend, Leonardo da Vinci visited the

*C*YPRUS

village in 1481, and purchased a lace cloth for the main altar of the Milan Duomo. The *Lefkaritika* style was probably imported here in ancient times from Assyria. Much later, the Venetians brought it home, and set up their own lace industry on the island of Burano. In 1889 a local lace school was opened, and Lefkara lace regained much of its ancient renown.

Today you will see the Lefkarian women sitting along the street, in front of their homes, stitching away at great speed. The women's job is to stitch and their husbands' is to sell.

In Lefkara there is also a Lace and Silver Filigree Museum, open Monday-Saturday, 10am-4pm. Entrance fee.

Choirokoitia
3 miles past Lefkara, on the Larnaca-Limassol road, a road branches off north-westward to Choirokoitia, and the **Choirokoitia Archaeological Site**.

This is the site of the largest Neolithic (5800-3000 BC) settlement in Cyprus, sprawled out on a hillside along the Maroni river. Its people lived in stone and baked-mud huts, and buried their dead under the floor. They farmed the land, span and wove cloth, herded sheep and made earthen tools and effigies. Excavations uncovered signs of prime material, apparently imported from Asia Minor. The findings — amphor fragments, medallions, stone arrowheads and tools etc. — point to a very high level of culture. The site is open to visitors 7.30am-7.30pm (or until sunset in winter). Entrance fee. The local museum is only open on Tuesday, 7.30am-1.30pm.

Amathous
Five miles before reaching Limassol, on the right hand side of the road, you will see the ruins of Amathous, and just before them a large, modern hotel.

Amathous was once an opulent town, as witnessed by the ruins of its Acropolis, its Necropolis (cemetery), a Basilica, and further on, on the beach, the remains of its ancient harbour.

According to Greek myth, Amathous was founded in

C YPRUS

the 10th century BC, by Amathous, Heracles' son and Amathusa, mother of the local king. In one of their raids, the early Moslems sacked the town in the 7th century AD; in the 12th century, an earthquake completely destroyed it and it was never rebuilt. The excavations uncovered objects dating from the 10th centrury BC to the late Byzantine Era: bronze, silver and gold ornaments, coins and amphors. A gigantic six foot tall amphor was taken to the Louvres Museum in Paris. According to local lore, the amphor was illegally sold to France in 1862 by the Turkish Sultan. More recent digs have uncovered, among other objects, the upper torso of a statue of the Egyptian god Bes, now exhibited at the Limassol Museum.

Limassol

Limassol has a population of 120,000 and is the second largest town in Cyprus. Limassol is also Cyprus' main industrial and maritime centre. Its ancient name was "Nemessos". Here Richard the Lionheart weded Berengaria of Navarre and crowned her Queen of England. Over the centuries the town was repeatedly invaded and conquered from the sea.

Although Limassol is a busy industrial centre today, tourists only pass through on their way to more attractive sites. This is perhaps the reason why it has been able to maintain the traditions of Cypriot life. Nevertheless, quaint old boutiques and dark smoky inns are rapidly changing into modern shopping centres and restaurants.

How to get there

By Sea: Limassol is the main seaport of the island. As we have already mentioned ("How to reach Cyprus"), several shipping lines reach Limassol from Italy, Greece and Israel. The new harbour is in the southern section of the town. No.1 buses and the ubiquitous taxi services connect the harbour with the town centre.

By Land: Buses reach Limassol from all over the island, and stop at one of three main bus stations. The *KEMEK* buses have their terminal at the Enoseos and Eirinis Sts., north of the castle and not far from the centre and the sea. They include the Nicosia-Limassol line, the Pafos-Limassol and the Polis-Pafos-Limassol lines. For timetable and other information; call tel. 05-363241.

The *Kellenos* lines (tel. 05-362670) have their terminal at the corner of Araouzou and Hadjipavlou Sts. and they travel to Larnaca and to Agia Napa. The third bus station is used by most urban lines, and is on Andreas Themistokleu St., in the centre of town.

Limassol is also connected to the major island towns by a network of shared-taxi lines. They are faster and more frequent but twice as expensive as the buses. The shared-taxis have their terminals at 49 Spyrou Araouzou St. (*Kypros*, tel. 05-363979), or at 21 Thessalonikis St. (*Karydas* and *Kyriakos*, tel. 05-362061).

Urban transportation
The Central bus station is very central indeed, and the urban network connects it with Limassol's periphery and suburbs. There are also several private taxi stands near the station. Limassol is very crowded, its streets are narrow, parking is scarce and traffic is very slow.

Tourist services
The CTO office is at 15 Araouzou St., tel. 05-362756. Opening hours: September-May, Monday-Saturday 8.15am-1.45pm; Monday and Thursday also 3-5.30pm. June-August, Monday-Saturday 8.15am-1.30pm, Monday and Thursday also 4-6.15pm.

A CTO Branch Office operates at Dassoudi Beach (tel. 05-323211), the Limassol resort zone. Same opening hours.

The CTO branch in the harbour opens on arrival of passenger ships.

At the CTO offices you will be able to obtain a Limassol map and various written information. The office staff will also assist you with hotel reservations and travel information.

At Limassol you will find branches of all the main **car hire** agencies. *A. Petsas*, *Hertz* and *Avis* are on the Nicosia road; *Europcar* is closer to the city centre.

Hertz: Nicosia Road, G3 Anza Court, tel. 05-323758.
Avis: Nicosia Road, Kean Factory, tel. 05-324192.
Europcar: 28 Oktovrio St., 4B Blue Sea House, tel. 324025-28.

A.Petsas: Nicosia Road, tel. 05-323672.

Another local car-hire agency, smaller than the island-wide *A. Petsas*, is the *Andy Spyrou* company, with branches also at Pafos and Nicosia. Its offices are on 38-40 Omonia Ave., tel. 05-371441. If you have reserved your car in advance, a company driver will meet you, keys in hand, at the gate of the Limassol harbour.

Bicycle hire is at *Andreas Aristidou*, 1 Leontion Machera, tel. 05-364145.

All major Cyprus **banks** have branches in Limassol. The *Bank of Cyprus* has several branches, most of them downtown, between Spyrou Araouzou St. and Gladstonos and Navarinu. Money changing and other tourist services are also provided in the afternoon at the harbour and at the Agiou Andreou St. branches.

The main post office is on Archiepiskopou Kyprianos St., and the T&T office (open Monday-Saturday, 7am-midnight) is not too far, on Markou Botsarsi St.

Accommodation
As everywhere else in Cyprus, Limassol's cheapest hotels are also the most central ones. Luxury hotels are found along the eastern beaches, and on the Larnaca and Nicosia roads, together with several modern apartment hotels.

5-star
Amathus Beach: near the Amathus archaeological site, 5 miles from town, tel. 05-321152. Relatively expensive, but very well equipped; private beach.
Limassol Sheraton: at Amathus, 6 miles from town, tel. 321100. Outstanding services, also including a private beach.
Other 5-star hotels are the *Apollonia Beach* (Potamos Yermassogias, tel. 05-323351) and the *Poseidonia Beach* (Nicosia Road, tel. 05-321000); they are both east of town, toward Nicosia; very good services, if less ostentatious; their prices are somewhat lower.

LIMASSOL

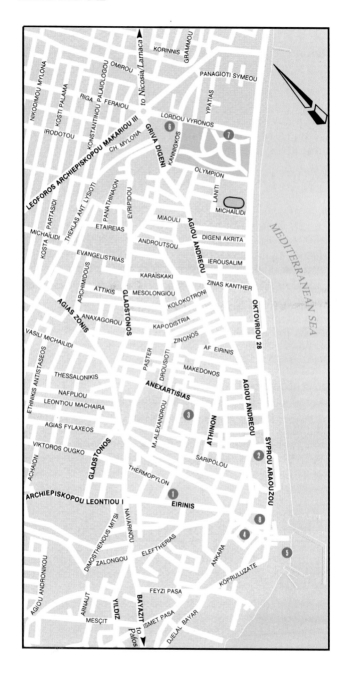

C YPRUS

4-Star
Churchill Limassol: 28 Oktovriou St., tel. 05-324444. Closer to 5 star both in prices and services. In the eastern suburbs. Private beach, pool and sauna.
Curium Palace: Vyronos St., tel. 05-363121. Central — and cheaper. Swimming pool, but no private beach.
Elias Beach: Amathous, 6 miles east of town, tel. 05-325000.
Limonia Bay: near the *Amathus Beach* hotel, tel. 05-321023. Very attractive prices.

3-Star
Adonia Beach: Amathous, tel. 05-321111. With a private beach, and very attractively located near the archaeological site.
Ariadne: 333, 28 Oktovriou St., tel. 05-359666. Within the eastern town limits. More expensive than the *Adonia Beach*. Swimming pool, but no beach.
Alasia: 1 Haydar St., near Makarios Ave., at strolling distance from the town centre, tel. 05-371747. Swimming pool.
Astir: 142 Anexartisias St., tel. 05-362161. Central.

2-Star
Pefkos: a stone's throw from the town centre, 86 Misiaoulis Kavazoglou St., tel. 05-377077. Swimming pool; room air-conditioning an extra.
Chez Nous Sunhotel: on Potamos Yermassogias St., tel. 05-323033. East of the town centre. Swimming pool and standard services.

Index
1. *K.E.M.E.K.* Terminal
2. *Lefkaritis* Terminal
3. Central Bus Station
4. Limassol Castle
5. Old harbour
6. Limassol Archaeological Museum
7. The zoo
8. CTO office

Inexpensive hotels

Le Village: 220 A. Leontiou St., tel. 05-368126. 500 yards west of the town centre.

Panorama: 36 Pavlos Melas St., tel. 05-364.667. Central; closes for the winter and re-opens in May.

Downtown, between Zinonos and Anexartisias Sts. there are some small (10-20 rooms) very inexpensive hotels; for those who are on a rather strict budget we will mention the following:

Acropole: 21 Yeorgiou Malekidi St., tel. 05-362706.
Astoria: 13A Yeorgiou Malekidi St., tel. 05-362.708.
Rose: 50 Zinonos St., tel. 05-362299.
Some of them are open only for the summer season.

Guest Houses

Arizona: 31 Mesolongiou St., tel. 05-364862.
Excelsior: 35 Anexartisias St., tel. 05-353351.

Youth Hostel: The only hostel is on 120 Ankara St. (tel. 05-363749), just behind the castle. Open all year, office hours 7.30am-11pm.

Apartment Hotels

Azur 2: A Class. Potamos Germasogia, tel. 05-322667. East of the town centre; studio apts. and 1 room suites; swimming pool; relatively expensive.

Renanda: A Class. Amathous, tel. 05-321133. 1-2 room suites. Air-conditioning and room TV are extras. Swimming pool.

Atlantica: B Class. Potamos Germasogia, tel. 05-321141. Rather far from the town centre; 1-2 room suites; swimming pool.

Chrielka: B Class. 7 Olympion St., tel. 05-358366; central.

Twiga: B Class. 114 Makarios Ave., tel. 05-367236. Very central, and relatively inexpensive.

Restaurants

Limassol has lots of *meze* restaurants, specially in the centre and in the eastern quarter.

Jack's Pizza Place: pizzas and spaghetti, has two branches: 15 Heraclis Michaelides St. (tel. 366424) and 144 Griva Digeni St. (tel. 324921).

Canadiana Pizza & Spaghetti is at 235H Makarios Ave., tel. 375555.

At 33 Stasinou St. (tel. 357387) you will find an Arab cuisine restaurant.

Santa Barbara Beach is a fish restaurant on the road to Amathous (tel. 321046); also bar, snack bar and café; relatively expensive, but its *grilled Haloumi* is outstanding; also excellent wines.

Psaropoulia is another Amathous fish and seafood restaurant, near the *Amathus Beach* and *Avenida* hotels; tel. 321494.

Mandarin is an excellent Chinese restaurant, in front of the *Castle* hotel, in the eastern quarter; Profili Elia St., tel. 325670.

M, on the Dassoudi Beach, offers both local and international menus. It is on the grounds of the *Drakos* apartment hotel, 47 Georgiou Ave., tel. 321508.

Scotti Steak House, 38 Sovliou St., corner of Leoforos Makarious III (tel. 335173) is the place to go for an excellent steak.

Andreas & Costas Lada, Syntagmatos Sq., near the old harbour (tel. 365760), is a fish restaurant.

Lefieris Tavern is an outstanding *meze* restaurant, in the Germasogia village, 4 Agias Christinis St., tel. 325211. Authentic atmosphere, excellent mutton roast; reasonably priced.

Shopping

The main shopping areas in Limassol are on Anexartiatis and Agiou Andreou Sts. and Leoforos Makariou III Ave., which draws a semicircle around the whole centre of town, from coast to coast. Plenty of footwear and clothing, some electrical appliances and electronics.

There are also some first class jewelry shops; the most prestigious is *Leo Jewelry*, 4 Anexartiasis St., tel. 355277.

What to see

Limassol, as mentioned, has no claims to Cyprus' tourism. The main historic site is **Limassol Castle**, near the old harbour. It is a 12th century structure, restored at a later

The seaside promenade at Limassol

date by the Venetians. This is where Richard the Lionheart celebrated his wedding to Berengaria of Navarre.

The castle will not sweep you off your feet; in spite of its historical value, the structure today has very little to offer. It is open to visitors June-September, Monday-Saturday 7.30am-6pm and Sunday 10am-6pm. In winter, 7.30am-5pm, weekdays only. Entrance fee.

Back from the castle, turn to the **old harbour**. In the square, at the corner of Safi and Spyrou Araouzou Sts., you will find find a Thai restaurant, a good seafood spot, the *Old Harbour Fish Tavern — Ladas*, and the **Reptile House** (open 9am-7pm, tel. 372779, entrance fee).

From the old harbour proceed north-westward, along Spyrou Araouzou St. After a few hundred yards, turn left into one of the alleys which cross to the parallel Agiou Andreou St. Here, at No. 2, there is an attractive shopping centre, with a pleasant café under the arches.

CYPRUS

28 Oktovriou St. runs along the shore toward the eastern quarters. About a mile from the old harbour it reaches the city park, with a small zoo and an open air theatre. The **Limassol Archaeological Museum** is also located on Lordou Vyronos St. exhibiting a number of stone axes, knives and arrow heads, tools and fragments recovered from Amathous and other sites. The museum also has coins and jewels of different periods on show.

The museum is open to the public 7.30am-6pm on weekdays, (October-April only until 5pm) and 10am-1pm on Sunday. Entrance fee.

Wine and beer cellars
Limassol is Cyprus' main wine-producing centre. All the island's major cellars are here, and some are open to visitors. Enquire at the CTO for their timetables and addresses.

Beaches
The Dassoudi tourist beach is equipped with adequate services, restrooms and cafés. If you plan to visit other resorts, don't bother to stop here.

Night life
Limassol prides itself as a modern town. It vaunts many new hotels, apartment hotels, high-rises and restaurants. On Georgiou A. Potamos Yermasogias St., east of the promenade, are the *Caribbean Night Spot & Disco* (tel. 321968) and the *Triangle Disc* (tel. 323322).

Near the *Apollonia* hotel, north of the main road, is the *Mylos Disco*. At 50A Omonia St. you will find the pleasant *Ataliotis Costakis* pub.

There are 8 cinemas in Limassol.

Sports
There are tennis courts at several hotels, and also at the *Limassol Tennis Club* (3 Mesarias St., tel. 276787) and at the *Sporting Club* (11 Olympion St., Tsiflikoudia, tel. 359818).

There are three major diving clubs:

Aquarius Diving School: tel. 322042.
Seamasters: 54A Franklin Roosevelt, tel. 376787.
Ninos: 47-51 Spyrou Araouzou, tel. 372667.

At the Dassoudi beach you will also find a watersports centre.

Festivals and Fairs
Six weeks before Easter, Limassol celebrates a ten-day Carnival, with numerous entertainers and various amateur groups.

In September Limassol celebrates Dionysos' Wine Festival, jointly sponsored by the major wine and beer cellars.

The Limassol District
Akrotiri
A visit to the Akrotiri Peninsula, on a sunny day, will make a very pleasant car or bicycle ride. Leave town in the direction of Asomatos, passing through the Fassouri vineyards. At Fassouri, turn left to the **salt lake**, where flamingoes and other birds of passage come to winter. Twelve miles past the salt lake, you will come to the attractive **Lady's Mile** beach.

The Germasogia Dam
Another pleasant ride will take you to the Germasogia Dam. Leave Limassol on the Old Nicosia Road (not the highway). After 2.5 miles turn left to the large village of Germasogia. At the Dam, if you have a fishing permit (CYP 1; tel. 05-362470), you will be allowed to fish.

The Troodos Mountains
The road leaves Limassol northward, climbing gradually through the southern reaches of Troodos. A ride of about 30 miles will first take you to **Alassa** and Platres, and then to Troodos itself, the district capital. Even if you have a shorter trip in mind, you will find plenty of attractive picnic areas and scenic stops on the way.

C YPRUS

You can reach Troodos by a second, longer, but prettier, approach: leave Limassol on the Pafos road to Erimi, a small village at Episkopi's gates. Visit the **Kolossi Castle** (see "From Limassol to Pafos"). At **Erimi** turn northward, through Kantou and Agios Amvrosios.

After 12 miles the road changes into a track; after 3 miles of bumps and jolts you will find yourself in **Omodos**, surrounded by what was once Sir John de Brie's Vineyard. August is the time of the local Wine Festival, and on September 14 there is a colourful religious procession to the Stavros Monastery, which houses icons and wooden effigies. Three miles beyond Omodos you will come to **Kato Platres**, and, after a left turn, to **Foini**. Here the local villagers make unusual, old-fashioned earthenware by hand. The local stream teems with excellent trout; the local mountain wine is more than palatable. Now back to Kato Platres, then to **Pano Platres**, and from there again to Limassol.

You may also enjoy a short visit to **Agros**, an attractive summer resort north of Limassol, on the **Phyla**, **Palodeia** and **Kalon Chorion** road.

Useful addresses and phone numbers
Limassol's prefix: 05.
First Aid, Police and Fire Brigade: 199.
Hospital: corner of Leontiou and Gladstonos Sts., tel. 363111.
KEMEK Bus Lines: corner of Enoseos and Erinis Sts., tel. 363241.
Acropolis taxis: 49 Spyrou Araouzou St., tel. 366766.
CTO: 15 Spyrou Araouzou St, tel. 362752.
Tourist Centre: Dassoudi beach, tel. 323211.

From Limassol to Pafos
The Limassol-Pafos road is pleasant, wide and well kept. It runs along the seashore, and passes through several interesting scenic points and historic sites. The first, less than 10 miles off Limassol, is **Kolossi**, the village that gave its name to the most famous castle on the island.

Kolossi Castle
This imposing structure was built in 1191. Exactly one hundred years later the castle became the property of the Order of Saint John of Jerusalem, in whose care it remained for 250 years. It stands in the middle of what · is probably the most fertile district on the whole island, to which we owe the splendid *Commandaria* wine. In 1570 the Turks conquered the castle — but did not stop growing and producing its wines for centuries. The district was also the main grower of sugar cane, and exported large quantities of it to Europe. The ancient sugar-mill can still be seen, at the foot of the castle walls.

The castle itself was fully restored in 1933. It has three levels, serviced by a steep winding staircase. In the lobby you will see a picture of the Crucifixion. On the first floor are the kitchens and on the upper floor is the commander's hall. The castle is open to visitors 7.30am-7.30pm (or, in winter, until sunset). Entrance fee.

Five miles beyond the Kolossi turnoff is **Episkopi** and the local archaeological site of **Pamboula** (14th-11th century BC ruins and several Bronze Age tombs).

Between Episkopi and the beach is the Byzantine Chapel of **Agios Hermogenis**, with its much more ancient stone Cemetery (11th century BC to the Roman Peiod). In one of the tombs a gold sceptre was found, now exhibited at the Cyprus National Museum of Nicosia.

Curium (Kourion)
Five miles past Episkopi the road climbs to Curium, a settlement founded more than three thousand years ago by Mycenean immigrants. According to Herodotos, the settlement was founded by Kourieus, son of King Kineras. During the wars between the Greek settlers and the Persians, its Greek chieftain Stasanor betrayed the town to the Persians without a struggle. Later, under Alexander the Great, Curium became one of the emperor's major strongholds. In the 4th century AC the town was repeatedly damaged by earthquakes, and in the 7th century AD it was completely razed by the Arabs.

Antiquities in Curium

Its ruins were discovered toward the end of the 19th century, but the first serious excavations began only in 1933. One of the most important structures is undoubtedly the theatre, with its fantastic view of the beach and the surrounding hills. It dates from the 2nd century BC. It was restored and strengthened three centuries later and destroyed by a 5th century quake. The theatre was fully restored in 1961, boasting two thousand seats, from which one enjoys one of Cyprus' best views of the Mediterranean. During the summer it presents a programme of Greek tragedies and other plays. Also noteworthy are the mosaic floors and the Roman baths.

The **Mosaic of Achilles** is the most interesting of the floors. The visit will not be complete without a stop at the **Roman gladiators' house**, or a good look at the **aqueduct** and at the ruins of the early Christian **basilica**. And at every corner you will see scores of Corinthian capitals and columns.

The site is open daily, 7.30am-1.30pm in summer, and in winter until 2pm. On Saturday it closes at 1pm. Entrance fee. The museum opens its doors only on Tuesday, same hours.

Two miles beyond Curium on the Pafos road, you will come to the **Ylatis Sanctuary of Apollo**, which for more than ten centuries (from the 8th BC to the 4th AD) was a very influential local centre of power. Near the ruins of the sanctuary you will also recognize the structure of a 2nd century stadium and one of the very earliest Christian basilicas. The sanctuary of Apollo is open to visitors 7.30am-7.30pm in summer, and until sunset in winter.

On the northern side of the Pafos Road you will see the village of **Sotira**, on the slopes of a hill. It was built around the ruins of a very ancient (third millennium BC) settlement, which has not undergone much research.

To Pafos
After Curium the road leaves the coastline and cuts into

the interior. Back to the coast after 12 miles, you will arrive at **Petra tou Romiou**, a majestic boulder high above the sea, the mythical birthplace of the goddess Aphrodite.

Six miles further on (and only 6 miles from Pafos itself) is **Palaia Pafos** (Old Pafos), near the village of Kouklia. According to legend, Old Pafos was founded by Kinares, and destroyed by an earthquake in the 12th century BC. Later, when King Agafanor was returning from the Trojan War, his ships were swept ashore by a storm, and Pafos was rebuilt by the survivors. According to some estimates, over 20,000 lived here, working the copper mines and trading with Greek sailors. In the 4th century BC the last King of Pafos, Nikokles, founded New Pafos. The old city was gradually abandoned, surviving only as Aphrodite's sacred grounds. The Goddess' annual festival was, until the advent of Christiendom, one of the major events of the region, and indeed of all Greece, with tens of thousands of pilgrims dancing and making merry for several days.

The excavation of the **Sanctuary of Aphrodites** began in 1988; work went on sporadically for more than a century, and is still going on. The various strata cover a period from the 9th century BC to the 5th century AD.

In addition to the sanctuary, the digs also uncovered a wall and the foundations of a large building, perhaps a hostel for incoming pilgrims. The Sanctuary is open in summer 7.30am-7.30pm, and in winter until sunset. Entrance fee. The local museum is only open on Tuesdays, 7.30am-1.30pm.

Near the Police Post of **Kouklia** you will see the ruins of a Roman structure. It has a unique mosaic floor, which is now exhibited at the **Kouklia Museum** together with several amphors and other findings. More precious findings, including ancient gold coins and jewels, can be viewed at the **Nicosia Archaeological Museum**. The 1987 digs uncovered many additional gold ornaments and objects, and a rare bronze basin decorated with an 11th century BC Greek inscription.

On arrival in Pafos you will pass through the village

Along the road from Limassol to Pafos

of **Geroskipou**, famous for its "Turkish Delight". It also vaunts a small Art Museum (see "Around Pafos").

Pafos

Pafos is the capital of Cyprus' western region. It has a population of 20,000, most of whom are employed in various branches of tourism. Pafos is very popular with tourists, and specially with German and Scandinavian tourists. Among its attractions are its old harbour, its ancient mosaic floors, and its modern restaurants and hotels, set out along the seaside promenade. And the main shopping lane, which runs parallel to the promenade, is the ideal tourists' marketplace.

Nea Pafos (New Pafos) was founded in the 4th century BC, 10 miles west of Old Pafos. Only centuries later the new city began to grow until it practically replaced its old namesake, and, with the decline of Salamis, bacame the capital of western Cyprus. When St. Paul brought the message of Christ to its people in the year 45, he was first lashed and imprisoned. He ended up, however, converting the Roman governor himself along with most of the population.

Pafos was destroyed twice, first by a 1st century quake, and then, in the 7th century, by Arab raiders.

In the 13th century, under the de Perpignans, Pafos became a bishopric seat, but even this did not prevent its people from leaving their town to seek more attractive dwellings in the neighbouring hills. Thus Ktima gradually replaced Pafos as the main regional centre. Today Ktima has been practically incorporated into Pafos itself. This is where the city administration is located, side by side with all major office buildings.

The Leoforos Apostolou Pavlou (St. Paul) Ave. connects Ktima with New Pafos (also known as Kato Pafos, or Lower Pafos), where the town's best hotels and residences, tourist beaches and archaeological sites are located.

How to get there

By Air: Although Pafos is only a small town, it has its own airport, which serves hundreds of thousands of European tourists, coming in by dozens of charter flights from Western and Northern Europe. The airport is less than 10 miles from town, but is only connected to the old and new city by private "special" taxis; there are no regular buses as of yet.

By Sea: Regular shipping lines do not dock at Pafos harbour, but hundreds of private yachts frequent the local Marina.

By Land: The *KEMEK* bus lines (tel. 06-234255) connect Pafos with all main centres on the island: Limassol, Larnaca (via Limassol) and Nicosia (via Limassol). Buses leave Limassol for Pafos approximately every three hours.

The *KEMEK* Terminal is in Ktima, on Fellahoglou St.. At the corner of Athinas and Thermopylon Sts. is the bus stop for Lower Pafos.

The Pafos-Polis line belongs to the *Fontana Amoroza Bus Company*; its buses leave every hour on the hour (but you are advised to make confirmations by phone at tel. 06-236740 in Pafos, or tel. 06-321115 in Polis).

Special buses connect Pafos with Coral Bay and with Pyrgos (*ALEPA* bus company, tel. 06-234410).

Shared-taxi lines (*Karydas* and *Kypros* company) run from Pafos to Polis and Limassol and vice versa.

Tourist services

The **CTO** Office is located at 3 Gladstonos St., tel. 06-232841. The airport branch (tel. 06-236833) opens according to incoming flight time tables. At the CTO you will find lots of information as well as hotel reservation services.

Along the promenade (Poseidonos Ave.), you will find the branches of 4 different **banks**, including the *Bank of Cyprus*, generally open for money changing also in the afternoon. The airport bank branch is open around-the-clock.

The Lower Pafos Post Office is on Agiou Antoniou

St., slightly north of the *Dyonisos* hotel and the abovementioned branch of the *Bank of Cyprus*. The Main Post Office is in Upper Pafos, on Leoforos Evagora Pallikaridi St..

Car hire
Here are the addresses of local car hire branches:

Europcar: 77 Poseidonos St., tel. 234149.
Hertz: 54A Apostolou Pavlou Ave., tel. 233985.
A. Petsas: Apostolou Pavlou Ave., tel. 235522.
Louis Self Drive: 9 Makarios Ave., tel. 233320-9.

Bicycles and motorbikes
S.P. Christoforou: Poseidonos St., across from the *Sodap* Cellars, tel. 237115.
Pelican rentals: 3 Phitagorou St., near the *Apollo* hotel, tel. 234303.

Accommodation
All Pafos hotels and apartment hotels are located in Lower Pafos, and are very close to one another. The best hotels are lined along the beach.

During the summer season (June through October) advance reservation is a must.

5-Star
Imperial Beach: on the Poseidonos promenade, tel. 06-236011.

4-Star
Annabelle: also on the promenade, tel. 06-238333. Excellent services; private beach; relatively high-priced.
Cypria Maris: at the far end of the promenade, tel. 06-238111. Somewhat cheaper; all-year (heated) swimming pool — and (unheated...) private beach.

3-Star
Aloe: promenade, tel. 06-234000. Not really close to the sea, and no private beach; large swimming pool, quiet and relaxing atmosphere; cottage style building; reasonably priced.
Dionysos: 1 Dionysos St., tel. 06-233414. Central. No private beach; swimming pool and scenic view of the sea.

PAFOS

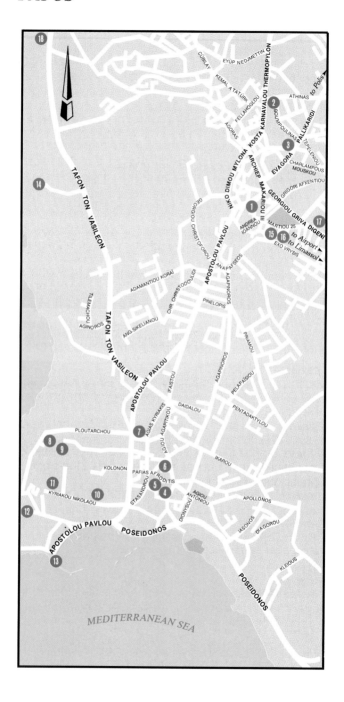

CYPRUS

Cynthiana Beach: 5 miles north of Pafos, on Coral Bay Road, tel. 06-233900. Private beach and swimming pool.

2-Star
Apollo: Leoforos Apostolou Pavlou, between Ktima and Lower Pafos, tel. 06-233909. 500 yards from the beach; swimming pool.
Theofano: Danaes St., on the road to the airport in eastern Lower Pafos, half a mile from the centre of town. Swimming pool.

Inexpensive hotels and pensions
Kinyras: Ktima, 89 Leoforos Makariou III, tel. 06-232522.
Pafos Palace: Ktima, 10 Griva Digeni St., tel. 06-232346.
Pelican Inn: 102 Apostolou Pavlou Ave., tel. 06-232827.
At Cedar Valley there is a pleasant, inexpensive pension (tel. 06-222338), recommended by local travel agents.

Youth hostel
Ktima, 37 Elftheriou Venizelou, tel. 06-232588, open all year; office hours 7.30-10am and 4-11pm.

Apartment hotels
Daphne: 3 Alkiminis, tel. 06-233500. A Class. Studio apts. and 1-2 room suites. Swimming pool, but no private beach, although situated by the sea.
Demetra: Artemidos St., tel. 06-234444. Central, studio apts and 1-2 room suites. A Class.
Mirofori: Constantias St., tel. 06-234311. Central, near the Post Office branch but not near the beach. Studio apts., 1 room suites; swimming pool. B Class.
Theseas: 1-3 Jasonos St., tel. 06-235511. Central, and

Index
1. CTO office
2. *K.E.M.E.K.* Terminal
3. *Fontana Amoroza* Terminal
4. St. Paul's Pillar
5. Chrysopolitissa Church
6. Frankish Bath
7. Agia Solomoni Catacombs
8. The lighthouse
9. Roman Audion
10. Saranta Kolones
11. House of Dionysus
12. Villa of Theseus
13. The Castle
14. Tombs of the Kings
15. Ethnographic Museum
16. Byzantine Museum

near the beach. Slightly higher priced than the *Mirofori*, 1-2 room suites. Swimming pool. B Class.

Camping
The Camping site is located at the Geroskipou beach, 2 miles east of the harbour. Space for 95 tents and trailers; services include showers, toilets, minimarket, snack-bar and electrical sockets. Open March to October, tel. 06-242277.

Restaurants
The promenade offers a wide choice of *meze* restaurants, all more or less similarly priced. At the old harbour restaurants (e.g. *Pelican*), you will eat at an open air table, with a startling sight of... sea-weeds.

Kyklamino is rather far off, but also far-out; worth the ride: on Pyramos St., tel. 06-237766.
Pafos Palace is a café restaurant on Kennedy Sq., tel. 06-232346.
Mediterranean Tavern and Restaurant, at 3 Agias Napas St., tel. 06-235684, serves as both an international and *meze* restaurant.
At 3-4 Poseidonos Ave. you will even find a pizza parlour and cafeteria (tel. 06-235816).

Shopping
Most shops are located on Makariou III Ave., in Ktima. The shopping facilities in Pafos leave much to be desired. The open market is at the north end of the avenue.

Opening hours are, in winter, 8am-1.30pm and 2.30-5.30pm; in summer 8am-1pm and 4-7pm. On Wednesday and Saturday afternoons most shops remain closed.

The *Cyprus Handicrafts Service* is located at the Agios Theodoros and Gladstonos Sts. corner; it offers a wide selection of local handicrafts.

Transportation
The city bus station. which connects the various sections of town, is located in Ktima, on the corner of Athinas and Thermopylon Sts.

What to see
Pafos is full of interesting sites, all in the lower, old city.

Lower Pafos
We will start at the intersection of the shopping lane which runs parallel to the promenade with Apostolou Pavlou St. Proceed eastward along the promenade to the first left turn (near the *Daphne Hotel*), onto Alkiminis St. Walk up and then make a second turn left. On your right you will see the well preserved early Christian **basilica**. You need a little bit of luck to visit it: it has no regular opening hours. An imposing Gothic church once stood near the basilica. It was destroyed during the 16th century. Here you will see **St. Paul's Pillar**. According to tradition, St. Paul was tied to it and lashed by the Roman governor of Pafos. Further on, in the same street, is the beautiful **Chrysopolitissa Church**. Next you will come to the **Frankish Bath**; only a few fragments remain of the old baths, but their discovery was of considerable archaeological importance. Now return to Apostolou Pavlou Ave., and turn right, to the **Agia Solomoni Catacombs**, which during the Byzantine Period were also used as a church.

Follow the avenue, and after the *Apollon* hotel turn right into the narrow Ploutarchou St., which climbs to the **lighthouse**. From here you will enjoy one of the best panoramic views of Pafos. A reconstructed 1st century **Roman Audion** is located near the lighthouse, today it serves as an open air dance and music centre. Turn south along the path, and the next east-west road will take you to **Saranta Kolones**, the ruins of a large Byzantine palace of the 7th century.

At the end of Kyriakou Nikolaou you will see a sort of large loft, where the incomparable floor fragments of the **House of Dionysus** are kept. These 4th century mosaics belonged to the residential palace of the Roman governor, and they shed light on various aspects of local daily life and depict the major figures of Greek mythology.

One of the mosaics depicts Dionysus (better known as Bacchus, the god of wine), erect on his panther-driven chariot and surrounded by a host of satyrs. Another mosaic illustrates the origins of wine: at one end Dionysus

Souvenirs awaiting the tourists

himself is happily sipping his godly nectar; at the other end two shepherds lie drunkenly at the feet of King Ikros, the first mortal taught by Dionysus the divine art of winemaking. Waking up from their drunken stupor, the two peasants, convinced that the king had tried to poison them, murdered the king on the spot. Other mosaics depict love and hunting scenes, duels and races. One shows a dying horse, falling prey to a panther's claws. Unique among all that violence is the idyllic scene of a vine harvest.

A Hellenistic mosaic of the 4th century BC was discovered, past the grounds of the palace, on its north side. The mosaic shows the two mythical monsters of Charybdis and Scylla of Homeric renown, lying in ambush in the waters of the Messina straits. Scylla's upper torso and face are those of a startlingly beautiful woman; but her other half is a scaled monstrosity, part fish and part crab-like.

The site is open to visitors daily, in summer 7.30am-7.30pm and in winter only until sunset. Entrance fee. The local museum is only open on Tuesdays, 7.30am-1.30pm.

The House of Dionysus

Near the House of Dionysos you will see the Villa of Theseus, also full of interesting mosaic floors. A round mosaic (which apparently was the floor of a round hall) illustrates Theseus' battle against the Minotaur (Chrete's terrible mythological monster), who kept guard over the Knossos Maze. The floor of the main hall depicts Achilles' birth, with his parents — Thetys and Peleos, witnessing his almost total immersion (with the fateful exception of his heel). Site and local museum follow the timetable of Dionysus' House. Entrance fee.

From the Villa of Theseus turn southward to the towering **Old Port and Castle**. Today Pafos' old port is completely submerged, probably since one of the frequent earthquakes that plagued the region in ancient times. In 1959 a team of British divers searched the area, recovering from the shallow seafloor several fragments and objects belonging to the old harbour. Today the site is marked by two large boulders. The small breakwater fort belongs to the de Lisignan Epoch (13th century AD). Destroyed by the Venetians, the fort was rebuilt by the Turks in 1586. It is open to visitors on weekdays, in summer

7.30am-1.30pm and in winter until 2pm; Saturdays only until 1pm. Entrance fee.

Along the old port are several restaurants and cafés, which provide perfect scenery for a welcome break and meal.

Rested and well-fed, turn eastward to the Apostolou Pavlou corner, where you started your walk. Now you may stroll eastward along the promenade, stopping to admire the crowds and the attractive shop windows.

The Tombs of the Kings
Approximately 2.5 miles north of the old port are the Tombs of the Kings (Tafon ton Vasileon). If it seems too long a walk, there is always the bus. Leave the promenade northward along Apostolou Pavlou Ave., and follow it to the road sign, whose arrow points left toward the site. The tombs are impressive enough to be worthy of kings — even if they are not. They are burial caves carved into the bedrock of the hill, and decorated with doric columns and capitals; they date from the 4th century BC, The site is open 7.30am-7.30pm in summer, and only until sunset in winter months. Entrance fee. Local museums only open on Tuesdays, 7.30am-1.30pm.

Ktima
Today Ktima — or Upper Pafos — is the district capital. In the past, it was the burial grounds for new Pafos — or lower Pafos. "Ktima" in Greek means "property".

Among this "property" are several small but interesting museums. The **Ethnographic Museum** is in Exo Vrisi, near the seat of the Pafos archbishopric. It contains a collection of costumes and other objects characteristic of Cypriot daily life over the centuries. Opening hours are 9am-1pm and 4-7pm on summer weekdays (June-September); the rest of the year the afternoon hours are 3-5pm. On Sunday, only 10am-1pm. Entrance fee. The **Archaeological Museum** of Pafos is on Georgiou Griva Digeni. It exhibits ancient Neolithic and Bronze Age idols; amphors from various periods; statues, statuettes and fragments from local digs and the statues of Dionysus and Esculapios from the House of Dionysus. Open in summer

7.30am-1.30pm and 4-6pm on weekdays (10am-1pm on Sunday); in winter, Monday-Friday 7.30am-2pm and 3-5pm, Saturady 7.30am-1pm and 3-5pm and on Sunday 10am-1pm only. Entrance fee.

The **Byzantine Museum** is at the archbishopric seat, not far from the Ethnographic Museum, on 25 Martiou St. (south of the city garden). It belongs to the greek-orthodox church. The museum's collection of icons is outstanding. Open June-September, Monday-Friday, 9am-1pm and 4-7pm (Saturday mornings only); the rest of the year afternoon hours are 3-5pm. Entrance fee.

Geroskipou

Three miles east of Pafos is the Cyprus home of *Loukoumia* (Turkish Delight) — the picturesque village of Geroskipou.

Its **Agia Paraskevi Church** is one of the best examples of Byzantine architecture in Cyprus. It is a five-domed structure of the 11th century, with each dome forming a separate chapel, with some beautiful and well-preserved 15th century frescoes.

An old residence houses the **Folklore Museum**, and contains a number of old looms, tools and woodwork. Open on weekdays, in summer 7.30am-1.30pm and in winter until 2pm (Saturday only until 1pm). Entrance fee.

The beach

The Pafos tourist beach is situated east of lower Pafos, towards the airport and towards Geroskipou. The hotels' private beaches occupy the strip below the promenade.

Night life

Night life in Pafos belongs to its tourists. Almost every 4-star hotel has its own disco. The most-popular is at the *Rainbow*, in upper Pafos (tel. 06-234044). But the major and most popular night life activity in Pafos remains... the traditional late evening stroll along the promenade, pausing for refreshments at one of the many cafés.

There are also three cinemas. The most popular pubs are the *Demetriou Georgios* (Agiou Antoniou St., tel. 235580), the *Pelican Pub* (30 Aphroditis St., tel. 235538), and the

Pafos — the port

The old castle

Jubilee Pub, a British establishment (35-38 Alkiminis St., tel. 237549) near the promenade and the *Daphne* hotel.

Sports
Pafos' watersports centres are located along the tourist beach. As for diving:

Annabelle Diving Centre: Pafos Beach, POB 136, Kato Pafos, tel. 06-233091.

Cy-Dive Diving Centre: Poseidonos Ave., Kato Phapos, tel. 06-234271.

Aloe Divers: Aloe hotel, Kato Pafos, tel. 06-234000.

Festivals
The main event is the sports and culture festival of *Pampaphia*.

Useful addresses and telephones
The Pafos prefix: 06.
Ambulance, police and fire brigade: tel. 199.
Hospital: Neofytou Nikolaidi St., Upper Pafos.
Police Post: Georgiou Griva St., Upper Pafos.
CTO: 3 Gladstonos St., tel 232841; airport branch, tel. 236833.
Bank of Cyprus: Dionysou Ave., lower Pafos, tel. 234231 — and at the airport, tel. 236962.

Around Pafos
Northward along the shore
The western coast roads are most suitable for bicycle rides. Take the Polis Road through the Tombs of the Kings, and turn left to **Coral Bay** and its beach. An excellent skin-diving spot, with a pleasant café. North of the bay is the village of **Pegeia** with some unusual fountains and waterjets on its main square.

Now leave the Polis Road and turn left (westward) to **Cape Drepanon**, with the ruins of the Agios Georgios Basilica and several old burial caves near a tiny fishermen's village. Three miles beyond the Cape is the **Lara Bay**, with one of Cyprus' best beaches.

Polis

Polis is a small town on the **Chrysochou Bay**, about 25 miles north of Pafos, with a startlingly beautiful fishing harbour. It was built on the site of the ancient Marion, a Hellenistic trade and cultural centre, prosperous thanks to its rich copper and gold mines. The Syrians changed its name to Arsinoe, a name it kept for several centuries, throughout the Byzantine Period. Today it is becoming one of Cyprus' summer resorts. It has several small and inexpensive hotels, both in town and along the western beach.

Elia is an A Class apartment hotel overlooking the sea, equipped with a swimming pool and good tennis courts (tel. 06-321011). The *Polis Camping* (tel. 06-321526) is in an eucalyptus grove by the sea, 500 yards from the town. It has 200 tent or trailer sites, and is fully serviced with showers, toilets, minimarket, first aid and electrical sockets. Small tents for hire. Open from March to November.

The *Arsinoe Water Sports* is a diving club — tel. 06-321216.

The site of the **Baths of Aphrodite** is less than six miles east of Polis. This is the mythical site where the goddess of Beauty used to bathe — in the "fountain of youth". We will not guaranty the effects, but who knows, you might give it a try — and enjoy the scenery: a small rocky pool hidden on the mountain-side, framed by fig trees and evergreens.

Near Cape Arnaoutis (a.k.a. Cape Akamas), 3 miles further on north-westward, is another legend: that of the **Fontana Amorosa** (The Fountain of Love); all those who drink its waters are supposed to fall instantly in love...

The Fountain of Love cannot be reached by car: you will have to board a boat from Latchi (west of Polis) or walk along the path crossing the rocky coast of the bay from the Baths of Aphrodite to the fountain. However, be warned: this area is used frequently by the Cyprus Army for its training exercises, and a military clearance must be obtained beforehand (for information, call the CTO).

C YPRUS

From Pafos to Troodos
There is no regular transportation service between Pafos
and Troodos. The following itineraries are, therefore, only
for private and rented cars, or by special taxi.

First Itinerary
This is the standard — and less exciting — route. It is
more direct, quicker but less rewarding. Leave Pafos on
the Limassol Road, and follow the Troodos road signs.
You may leave the coastal road towards Troodos slightly
before coming to Kouklia (old Pafos), in the direction of
Nikokleia and **Arsos**, or take the turnoff to **Prastion**. The
two segments join up before reaching Platres, on the
way to Troodos. There is little to see on the way, except
for the countryside, covered with vineyards and specked
with isolated farms and small hamlets. If you take the
Prastion route, after 12 miles you will come to **Omodos**,
whose vineyard used to belong to Sir John Brie, the
legendary crusader Prince of Galilee. August is the time
of the harvest festival here, and the village monastery
(Stavros Monastery) holds an annual procession on 14th
September.

A turn left will take you from Kato Platres, a few miles
beyond Amodos, to **Foini**, a small village famous for its
traditional handmade earthenware.

Second Itinerary
This route will take you from Pafos to Troodos along
winding asphalt lanes and mountain tracks, passing
through several interesting sites.

Leave Pafos on the Polis Road, crossing Tsada and
Mesogi. Slightly before Stroumpi turn right on the turnoff
to **Pano Panagia**. The road is difficult and bumpy; it climbs
three thousand feet to Pano Panagia, and offers some of
the most impressive sights on the island. Pause at one
of the mountain hamlets you cross, and see the Cypriot
mountain farmers at their millenary toil.

From Pano Panagia proceed on the eastward track,
towards the **Kykkos Monastery**. Road conditions are now
better, and you will be able to enjoy the view. It is a 20
mile drive from Pano Panagia to the Monastery, without

AROUND PAFOS

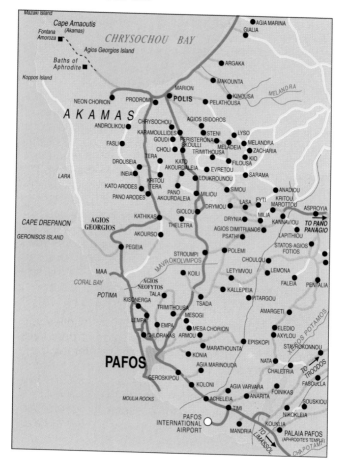

a single sign of human habitation. There are several turnoffs, each with its road-sign; there are other access roads to the monastery, but you will do well to follow the road-signs rather than any eventual suggestions by local "experts".

The Kykkos Monastery is more than 4000 feet, high and is

Kykkos Monastery

well worth a visit. The mountain air is clear but very cold; either come prepared, or accept the heavy mantles you will be offered at the entrance. In the courtyard you will see the mosaics illustrating the Crucifixion, the Nativity, the Resurrection and other miracles. This Monastery, the most ancient and richest in Cyprus, was built in 1100 and is dedicated to the Virgin Mary. In the main hall are two ancient icons, attributed to St. Lucas. An icon of the Virgin Mary, held in a special alcove, is believed to have miraculous powers. Archbishop Makarios III completed his ecclesiastic studies here; on his death, he was buried at Throni, two miles from the Monastery.

The road continues eastward to Pedoulas, where it turns southward, near the TV aerials of Mount Troodos (6150 f.) toward the Troodos.

The Troodos Mountains

The Troodos Mountains cover most of the central mass of Cyprus. Their higher peaks reach 6,000 feet; the highest, Mt. Olympos, is 6,403 feet high.

The capital of the district is **Troodos**, a small tourist village. The largest centre is Platres (6 miles from Troodos), with a wide selection of hotels, restaurants and shopping facilities. Platres climbes to a height of about 3,500 feet, on the southern slopes of Mt. Olympos, surrounded by pine forests. Platres is an excellent wintersports base, with convenient access to the Mt. Olympos ski-runs. The southern beaches are also not very far — half an hour ride by car or taxi. As the the local saying goes: "What is your choice: mountain-ski or water-ski?"

The winter-ski season generally lasts throughout January and February, and its main centre is Troodos. Summer tourism is also very popular (based mainly in Platres): the weather is pleasantly cool, and the forest paths and mountain climbs attract droves of European tourists.

Average temperatures in February reach about 40 F; in August temperatures rarely climb above 85 F.

The mountains are peppered with old monasteries; some of these go back to the Byzantine period; the oldest is the Peristerona Monastery which is more than 8 centuries old!

Transportation
A private car is very convenient indeed: there are no shared-taxi lines and no local buses. The carless visitor will have to manage with inter-urban bus stops, special taxis, and good walking shoes.

From Nicosia: the *KEMEK* (tel. 02-463154) bus leaves the Capital for Platres at 12.15am daily. The return trip goes through Kalopanagiotis and Pedoulas. The Troodos *Solea Bus* (tel. 02-453234) leaves Nicosia daily at 12am (from the Constanza Bastion stop, 200 yards from Eleftheria Sq.).

The *Solea Bus* company also runs the Nicosia-Kakopetria line (Kakopetria is 8 miles from Troodos). The *KEMEK* line also makes a daily run from Nicosia to the Kykko Monastery (see "From Pafos to Troodos"). For detailed information, call the Nicosia CTO.

From Limassol: The *Karydas* (tel. 05-362061) bus leaves for Platres at 12.45am. In July and August there may be additional runs; call the company for details. *KEMEK* also runs a daily bus to Platres; the return trip leaves Platres at 1.00pm for Prodromos, Pedoulas and Limassol. A special bus leaves Limassol at 11.45am for Agros, another mountain resort, east of Troodos.

There are no other regular bus connections with the Troodos mountains.

Tourist services

The mountain region is not densely populated, and its resorts are less popular than the beaches. Tourist services are also less developed. The closest hospital is in Limassol.

The only **CTO** branch is in Platres (open from mid-May to end-September, Main Square, tel. 05-421316). Here you will find a map of the region and a pamphlet with the itinerary of some interesting walks. The post office and a bank branch are also in the main square. None of the car-hire agencies has a branch in the mountains.

There are four other bank branches in the region: at Kakopetria, Pedoulas, Kyperounta and Prodromos.

Accommodation

There are several hotels in Platres, and others are located in the neighbouring villages. They are simple establishments, not as well equipped as their seaside counterparts, but they are generally pleasant, well serviced and clean. The only apartment hotel in the

THE TROODOS MOUNTAINS

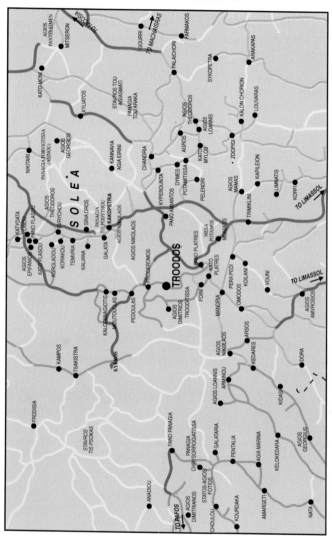

heights is in Platres (*Pauls*, B Class, 1-3 room suites, tel. 05-421425).

Following is a list of some of the local hotels:

The Troodos Mountains

Platres
All hotels are centrally located and are very close to one another.

Forest Park: tel. 05-421751. The only establishment offering not only heated rooms, but a heated pool as well (4 star).
Edelweiss: tel. 05-421335. 2-star; heated rooms.
Minerva: tel. 05-421731. One star; central heating (air-conditioning, room wireless, TV and telephone are extra) and a baby-sitting service.
Splendid: tel. 05-421425. One star, central heating.
Kalithea: tel. 05-421746. Very simple, 28 beds.
Mount Royal: tel. 05-421345. Very simple, 25 beds.

Troodos
Not a very wide selection:

Jubilee: tel. 05-421647. 2-star, central heating.
Troodos: tel. 05-421635. 2-star, central heating.

The **Youth Hostel** is located 400 yards from the village, on the Troodos-Nicosia Road (tel. 0r. 421649); open July and August. Office hours 7.30-10.30am and 4-12pm.

The **Camping-Site** is at little more than 1 mile from the village, on the Kakopetria Road. Equipped with showers, toilets, restaurant and bar, minimarket and first aid. Open from end-May to October. Tel. 05-421624. The nights are very cold; come well prepared.

Kakopetria
Makris: tel. 02-922419. 3-star, central heating.
Hellas: tel. 02-922450. 3-star, central heating.
Hekali: tel. 02-922501. 2-star, central heating.
Krystal: tel. 02-922433. 2-star, central heating.
Kyfissa: tel. 02-922421. Very modest.

Pedoulas
The Churchill Pinewood Valley: tel. 02-952221; services include central heating, pool, tennis courts and sauna (3-star).
Marangos: tel. 02-952657. No central heating; 2- star.
Jack's: tel. 02-952350, central heating; 1-star.
Central: tel. 02-952457. No central heating; 1-star.
Christy's Palace: tel. 02-952655; very modest.

Agros

Rodon: tel. 05-521201. 3-star, central heating and heated pool.
Vlachos: tel. 05-521330. 1-star.
Meteora: tel. 05-521331 very modest.

Restaurants

Most villages, including Troodos and Platres, have several *meze* restaurants; in Platres you will find more than ten along a strip of 200 yards of main road.

Wintersports

In winter, the Troodos mountain hotels turn into wintersport resorts: the Mt. Olympos slopes — and its ski-runs — are generally open for skiing throughout January and February, and often also in March. The runs are 7 miles from Platres, and can also be reached from Nicosia or Limassol in less than an hour.

The Cyprus Ski Club (POB 2185, Nicosia, tel. 02-441933), offers permanent and temporary membership subscriptions. The Mt. Olympos ski-runs are serviced by 4 ski lifts: two on the northern side and two along the southern Sun Valley. The northern (350 yard long) runs are for experienced skiers, the Sun Valley runs (150 yard only) are for beginners.

In Sun Valley you will also find a fully equipped wintersports sale and hire store. There are cafeterias and rest-rooms at all runs' ends.

Picnic sites

Along the hillsides of the Troodos mountains, there are many picnic grounds, most of them along the main roads and tracks. If you are motoring around, bring your own water and food, and select the best scenic spot on your itinerary.

Trips by car

The Northern Slopes

Leave Pano Platres southward, toward Kato Platres (not on the Limassol mainroad!). At Kato Platres take the side road to **Foini**, a small attractive village of traditional earthenware craftsmen. They work at their crafts without the help of modern technology.

From Foini take the northern track, after 2 miles it joines the Pano-Platres — Prodromos Road. Turn left toward Prodromos, and after little more than a mile you will see the **Trodhitissa Monastery**, which is in fact an 18th century church built on the foundations of a 13th century monastery. In the church you will find several icons and a statuette of the Virgin Mary, of Asian origins. The site is usually open from 12am-2pm. Do not enter wearing shorts (or immodest clothes!). Modest accommodation is available; no fixed payment is required, but donations are welcome.

Prodromos is a popular summer resort, on the slopes of the second highest Troodos peak. It is the seat of Cyprus' Forestry College.

From Prodromos, the road proceeds to **Pedoulas**, another summer resort, famous for its cherries. In the **Michael Archangel Church** you will find some interesting 15th century art works. The church is generally locked; keys are available next door on request. Pedoulas, Moutoullas and Kalopanagiotis are three villages perched on the slopes of the beautiful Marathasa Valley.

Seven miles east of Pedoulas is the famous Kykkos Monastery (see "From Pafos to Troodos").

Moutoullas is less than 1.5 mile north of Pedoulas; its church dates from the 13th century, and it has some very interesting frescoes. Its wooden roof is one of the earliest of its type; the church keys are available next door.

If you feel like visiting one more church, you may visit **Agios Ioannis Lampadistis**, in Kalopanagiotis, less than a mile further north. This church, which was also a former monastery, has some interesting 13th-15th century frescoes. Keys can be obtained either at the monastery, or in the house next to the bridge. The village is also famous for its sulphur springs. The next villages, Galata and Kakopetria, are further down the mountain slopes, in

One of many churches in the Troodos Mountains

the Solea district. You will find a turnoff to **Linou** about 7 miles from Kalopanagiotis.

Past Pano Flasou and Evychou the side road joins up with the Nicosia-Troodos main road. Turn right, and after a 4 mile ride southward, you will come to **Galata** and **Kakopetria**, two pleasant villages, each with its Byzantine church.

In fact, Galata has no less than three churches: the **Panagia Theotokos Church** (or Church of the Angel), a 12th century structure, decorated in the interior with 16th century frescoes; the **Panagia Podithou Church** (built in 1512) and the **Agios Sozomenos Church**, also a 16th century building with post-Byzantine frescoes. The keys can be found with the priest (enquire at one of the local cafés).

Beyond Galata you will reach Kakopetria, where you may turn off southwestward (for less than two miles) to the **Agios Nicolaostis Stegis**, another church built on the foundations of an earlier monastery. This is one of the most striking churches in Cyprus, with several 11th-

15th century frescoes. Open Monday-Saturday 9am-4pm; Sunday only from 9.30am.

Leave Kakopetria on the main Nicosia-Troodos Road, and you will be soon back at Troodos and Pano Platres..

East of Troodos

This itinerary will take you from Pano Platres to the eastern Troodos Plateau and back.

Leave Pano Platres on the main road, turning left toward Kakopetria; about half-way to the village, turn right following the road signs to **Kiperounta**, 3 miles away. Cross this rather large village and proceed to Chandria, and then further on to **Lagoudera**. Here you will find the 12th century **Panagia tou Araka Church**, one of the most famous churches in Cyprus.

Turn back from Lagoudera through Polystipos and **Alona**. Having crossed Alona, turn left to **Platanistasa**. Two miles past this village is the **Stavros tou Agiasmati Church**, with several 15th century frescoes.

Return to the Alona turnoff and proceed eastward through Fterikoudi and Askas to **Palaichori**, a village renowned for its pork sausages (*loukanica*) and its smoked pork (*chiromeri*). After sampling these delicacies, you will probably be ready to visit two more interesting churches: the **Panagia Chrysopantanassa** (16th century) and the Sotiros Church (15th century).

The Nicosia Road now turns north-eastward to Apliki, and, slightly off to your right, Gourri and Lazanias, where the **Machairas Monastery** is hidden.   ·

This monastery is situated at almost 3000 feet, on the eastern slopes of the Troodos Mountains, in a deep pine tree forest. It was founded in the 12th century as the receptacle of a holy icon of the Virgin Mary, found pierced by a sword (in Greek, sword - machaira), by two local monks.

In 1892 the building was almost completely destroyed by fire, and very little remains of its legendary treasures. After the fire it was rebuilt, and become famous once again in

1957. Gregoris Afxendiou, one of Colonel Grivas' Eoka fighters (see "History"), who was hiding on the monastery grounds, was discovered by the British, and to avoid being taken prisoner he burnt himself to death.

The monastery is open to visitors, and even provides accommodation (quite pleasant, and very convenient as a starting point for interesting forest walks).

The road from Machairas to Nicosia passes through the archaeological site of Tamassos (see From Troodos to Nicosia).

If you would rather go back towards Palaichori and Troodos, you will have the opportunity to visit **Agros**, one of the best mountain resorts. Here a side road will take you northward to **Chandria**, and from there to Kyperounta and Troodos or Pano Platres.

Mountain Walks

The CTO has selected several interesting mountain walks for you. Each itinerary is outlined on a map and described in a pamphlet; each pamphlet also contains a chapter specially for birdwatchers. This interesting material is available at the Platres CTO office.

There is also a specialized and richly illustrated guide of the region, *Landscapes of Cyprus*, by Daniel Geoff, published by Sunflower Books.

We shall briefly outline some of the itineraries.

The **first** ia also the longest: more than 6 miles (a 3-4 hour walk) on the Troodos-Prodromos Road; it climbs from Troodos up Mt. Olympos and to the TV aerials at its peak.

Leave Troodos and follow the road for 2 miles to the picnic site. Don't follow the arrow sign to **Mt. Olympus**, but carry on to Chromion; the direct path, indicated by the arrow, is steep, difficult and much more demanding. You will find several observation points on the way: the first toward Limassol and Platres; another, closer to the summit, overlooks the Kykkos Monastery, Prodromos and

Machairas Monastery

Throni (where the tomb of Archbishop Makarios III is located).

From here, if you feel up to it, you may climb to the top of Mt. Olympos. At the Troodos-Prodromos Road, turn right onto the mountain path that leads to the top.

The **second** itinerary leaves Troodos south-eastward and ends at one of the most striking observation points in the whole region. It is less than a 4 miles walk (but don't forget the way back...). There are some benches just a few minutes' walk from Troodos, near an observation point overlooking Mt. Olympos. Cross the Pano Amiantos (Asbest) Mines; a little further on you will come to the observation point, which has a spectacular view of the mines, the port of Limassol, the Salt Lake and several villages. It is also a good spot for a picnic, equipped with pine-wood tables and benches. Enjoy your rest, your picnic — and the view, and having rested, walk back to Troodos along the same path.

The **third** itinerary is a short walk (little more than a mile!) along the Kryos Potamos stream to the **Caledonia Falls** (no relation whatsoever to the Niagara Falls...). Start south-westward from Troodos, on the Platres Road (not far from the summer cottage of the President of Cyprus). On the way down you will see a signpost "500 meters — Nature Trail Caledonian". The trail is pleasant, the vegetation impressive, and the view is spectacular. You may either turn back, or proceed along the path to Platres, leading back to Troodos. From here you may catch a bus or hitch a ride. We don't advise climbing back: the path upward to Troodos reaches 2,000 feet in less than a mile!

All itineraries start from Troodos; if you are staying in Platres, you should first get a ride into Troodos.

From Troodos to Nicosia

The distance from Troodos to Nicosia is 50-65 miles, according to the different routes.

The main road is rather good, and leaves Troodos in an

easterly direction to Pano Amiantos, turning northward to Kakopetria and Galata. Having climbed down the northern slopes, it continues straight to the Capital. If you are not in a hurry, turn right 9 miles after Galata (and 5 miles before Astromeritis) to **Nikitari**. You may expect a very bumpy drive. After 3 miles you will get to the **Assinou Church** (a.k.a. Panagia Forviotissa — 12th century), with the most striking Byzantine frescoes on the island. To visit the church, you will need the help of the Nikitari priest.

On approaching Nicosia you will come across a detour (indicated by clear road signs), since a segment of the main road is located within Turkish territory and cannot be crossed.

The longer, but more interesting route climbs down from the mountains through Palaichori and the Machairas Monastery (see "The Troodos Plateau"), continuing eastward to Nicosia.

If you wish to stop at the **Tamassos archaeological site**, turn right 6 miles past Palaichori toward Klirou. Cross the village and Malounta, turning right at Arediou toward Episkopeion and Pera. At Episkopeion turn right once more to Politikon, and you will find yourself beside Tamassos (see "Around Nicosia").

After the visit, turn back to Episkopeion and Pera. Less than one mile after Pera you will reach the Nicosia Road. Turn left at the last 9 miles of the ride to the capital.

Nicosia

Nicosia is the capital of Cyprus and its largest city and business centre. It has a population of 170,000. It is more modern and lively than the rest of the island. Nicosia is the seat of government and home to all major businesses, it also boasts the best shopping facilities in Cyprus.

The city is politically and historically divided: its northern section belongs to Turkish Cyprus. The border crosses its streets and alleys, and on many corners you will see small bunkers and guardposts manned with armed soldiers.

Historically, Nicosia is divided into an old city and a new city; but the political border splits the old city in two. The old city was once surrounded by a wall, only parts of which still remain. Its streets are but narrow alleys; its houses are old and rather neglected. Most buildings in the old city are protected by law, with plans for their periodical restoration. A small section (Laiki Yitonia — "The People's Neighbourhood") has already undergone restoration, and its narrow alleys, lined with small shops and restaurants, will give you an idea of what Nicosia was like three centuries ago. The new city spreads southward, with only an occasional high rise in its centre. The suburbs are wide residential quarters, with small cottages and private villas — and no apartment buildings. The main business centre is located in the new city, within the triangle formed by Stasinos, Makariou III and Evagora Sts.

Turkish Nicosia (or Lefkosa in Turkish) — is north of the dividing "Green Line". While the Greek new city, in the south, is modern and lively, Lefkosa is traditional in style and facilities. There are several Gothic structures, such as the Selimiye and the Bedesten Mosque or the Lapidary Museum. There are also a number of Ottoman style public buildings, such as the Arabahmet Mosque, the Büyük Han ("Great Inn"), the Kumarcilar Han (Gamblers' Inn) and the Sultan's Library.

NICOSIA

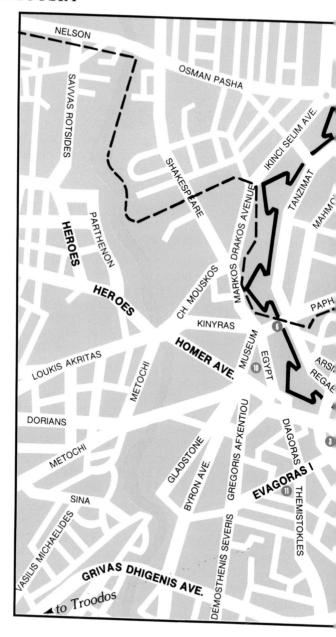

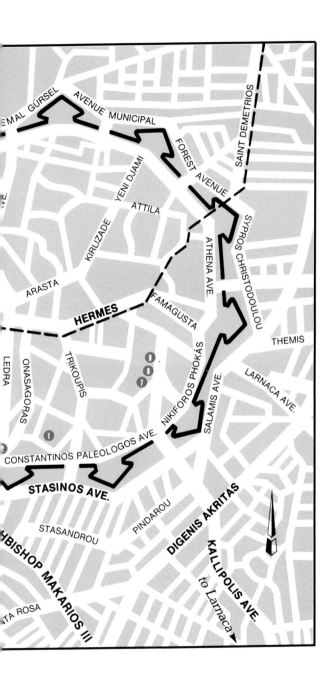

*C*YPRUS

The City Structure
The Old City, a rounded enclave in the centre of town, is clearly outlined by the remains of the ancient walls. Its southern section consists of the **Laiki Yitonia** neighbourhood — the heart of Nicosia, together with the three main shopping streets: Stasinos, Makariou III and Evagoras. West of this zone, the Pedieos river crosses the city from north to south. Beyond the river are the Engomi suburb, the *Ledra* hotel, and the airport (abandoned since the 1974 civil war). The so-called "Green Line", that divides the Greek and Turkish sections, is not green but nevertheless easily recognizable.

How to get there
By Air: Greek Nicosia has no operative airport today. The old one was partially destroyed in the 1974 war, and although it remains within the territory of Greek Cyprus, it has never been rebuilt.

Turkish Nicosia, or rather Lefkosa, is serviced by the small Ercan Airport, situated near the village of Tymvou, 6 miles east of the city.

By Land: The only Cyprus highway joins Nicosia

Index
1. Laiki Yitonia
2. Eleftheria Square
3. *K.E.M.E.K.* Terminal
4. *Kellenos* Terminal
5. Solomos Square Terminal
6. Paphos Gate
7. The Archbishopric Palace and the Agios Ioannis Cathedral
8. Museum of the National Struggle
9. Museum of Folk Art
10. Cyprus Museum
11. Museum of Modern Art

with Limassol, about 50 miles south-westward. The *KEMEK* bus line (tel. 02-463989 in Nicosia and tel. 05-363241 in Limassol) runs an hourly bus service between the two centres. The Nicosia terminal is on Leonidou St.

Several taxi companies also run shared and special taxis to and from Limassol:

Karydas: Limassol tel. 05-362555; Nicosia tel. 02-472525. *Inter Express Acropolis*: Nicosia tel. 02-466201.

The Larnaca main-road runs westward for 12 miles, and then joins the Limassol-Nicosia highway. These 12 miles are often packed with hundreds of private vehicles, trucks and buses, bumper to bumper. At peak hours it is a very slow and enervating drive.

Buses: *Kellenos*, Nicosia tel. 02-453560, Larnaca tel. 04-654890.

Taxi: Nicosia: *Karydas*, tel. 02-462269; *Kypros*, tel. 02-464811. Larnaca: *Kyriacos*, tel. 04-655100; *Inter Express*, tel. 04-652929.

Troodos is connected with Nicosia by two daily buses: the *KEMEK* bus (leaving Pano Platres at 6am, to Pedoulas and Nicosia); and the *Solea Bus* (6.30am from Troodos). Another *Solea Bus* line runs several times a day between Nicosia and Kakopetria.

The Agia Napa-Nicosia line offers a daily minibus ride — early morning from Agia Napa and mid-afternoon from Nicosia. The trip lasts about two hours.

Lefkosa — Turkish Nicosia — is connected by bus with Kyrenia (a 16 mile ride). Kyrenia is the Cypriot end of the Mersin (Southern Turkey) ferry service.

The only crossing open between Greek and Turkish Cyprus is the **Pafos Gate**, in the western section of Nicosia. Special visas are not required, but be prepared for lenghty and often unpleasant delays.

Transportation
The urban bus transportation network reaches almost every corner of the city; its main terminal is on Solomos

The Green Line

Sq, not far from Laiki Yitonia. Lots of private taxis cruise along all the main Nicosia streets, and can be hailed at will.

Tourist services

The CTO office (tel. 02-444264) is in Laiki Yitonia, in the Old City. Here you will find lots of written information on Nicosia and the rest of Cyprus, and the staff will assist you with information on cultural programmes and accommodation. The office is situated in a restored old residence, and it is not easily recognizable from the outside. Opening hours: September-May, Monday and Thursday 9am-5pm, Tuesday, Wednesday and Friday 9am-2.45pm, Saturday 9am-1.45pm; June-August, Monday and Thursday 9am-2.45pm and 4.30-6.30pm; Tuesday, Wednesday and Friday 9am-2.30pm and Saturday 9am-1.30pm.

The Main Post Office is also in Laiki Yitonia, across Constantinos Paleologos Ave., slightly west of the CTO.

Graffity at the Turkish side

The Telephone Office is on Marcos Dracos Sq., near the Pafos Gate.

The *Sunwash Laundrette* self service laundry is in Kaimakli, 7c Makarios Ave., tel. 02-432760 offering a 60 minute wash-and-dry service.

Bank branches are available everywhere; most common are the branches of Cyprus' two main banks: the *Bank of Cyprus* and the *Popular Bank*. The Makarios Ave. branches of both banks are also open for money-changing in the afternoon.

Car Hire
All major agencies have local branches in Nicosia.

Avis: 2 Homer St., tel. 02-472062.
Europcar: 7E Santa Rosa St., tel. 02-445201.
Hertz: Eleftheria Sq., tel. 02-477783.
A. Petsas: *Ledra* Hotel (tel. 02-457457) and 24 Pantelides Ave., tel. 02-462650.
Louis Self Drive Cars: 54-58 Evagoras St., tel. 442114.

Bicycle Hire: tel. 02-455487.

Accommodation
The capital offers a wide choice of hotels of all classes, but only one apartment hotel, the B Class *Lordos* (18 Sina St., Engomi — more than a mile from the centre of town — tel. 02-441039).

5-Star
Hilton: Leoforos Makarios III, tel. 02-464040. The only 5 star establishment, very central and ideally located, adjacent to the access road leading to the Limassol highway. Luxury services, including swimming pool, tennis courts and sauna.

4-Star
Churchill Nicosia: 1 Achaeans St., tel. 02-448858. Higher prices than most 4-star hotels. Centrally located, west of the Pedieos river. Services are adequate, but not comparable with 4-star hotels at seaside resorts.
Philoxenia: Eylenja Ave., tel. 02-499700. Off-centre, south of the *Hilton*; wide range of services, pool, sauna and tennis courts.
Ledra: Griva Digheni Ave., tel. 02-441086; west of the centre, quiet neighbourhood; swimming pool.

3-Star
Asty: 12 Prince Charles St., tel. 02-473021. 4-star prices; at one mile from the centre. No swimming pool.
Europa: 16 Alceos St., tel. 02-454537. West of the centre, near George Grivas Ave.
Excelsior: 4 Photiou Stavrou Pitta St., tel. 02-442062. Central, near Santa Rosa Ave., one of Nicosia main streets.
Kennedy: 70 Regaena St., tel. 02-475131. A modern building in the new city, outside the city walls. Roof swimming pool, with a splendid view of the city.
Lido: on the corner of Fylokyprou and Passicratoue Sts., tel. 02-474351. In the Old City, in the centre of Laiki Yitonia. Excellent site, depressing lobby and many unpleasant rooms.

2-Star
Averof: 11 Averof St., tel. 02-463447. East of the river, near the Green Line.
Nicosia Palace: 4-6 Pantelides Ave., tel. 02-463718. Within the old city walls.

Inexpensive hotels
Alexandria: 17 Trikoupi St., tel. 02-462160. No private bathrooms.
City: 215 Ledra St., tel. 02-463113.
Delphi: 24 Pantelides Ave., tel. 02-275211. Central, within the old city walls; basic.

Pensions
Alasia: 23 Pigmalion St., tel. 02-454384.
Femina: 114 Ledra St., tel. 02-465729.

The **Youth Hostel** is across the street from the *Asty* hotel, 1.5 miles from the centre, at 13 Prince Charles St., tel. 02-444808. Bus 27 from Solomos Sq. Open year round; office hours 7.30-10am and 4-11pm.

Restaurants
There are dozens of eating places in Laiki Yitonia, where you will find many *meze* restaurants, with or without *bouzuki* bands. Often a waiter is posted at the entrance, to entice passers-by to venture in. One of the best, at 4 Solonos St., is the *Byzantine Palace*. Try the *stiffado with couscous*. It is excellent!. George Grivas Ave. is lined with restaurants, always packed with a crowd of young Cypriots.

In the modern shopping centre situated at the corner of Makarios Ave. and Agias Elenis St. you will find the *Le Premier* café and restaurant (36 Agias Elenis St., tel. 02-365536), a very pleasant, but rather expensive lunch counter.

For cheap local cuisine and *meze* you may sample the *Kastri Tavern*, 9 Prokopian St., tel. 02-365677 — or the *Schistris Tavern*, 20 Aglantjias St., tel. 02-435460.
Chang's China is an excellent Chinese restaurant, 1 Acropolis St., tel. 02-458350. Open 12.30am-3.30pm and 7.30pm-00.30am; reserve your table by phone!

Music in Nicosia

Mignon, 38 Metochiou Kikkou St., tel. 02-445032 (across the street form the *Churchill* hotel, offers French and British cuisine.
Fish Kavouri is a seafood restaurant at 125 Strovolos Ave., tel 02-425153.
Cellari, 17 Corais St., tel. 02-448338 is a barbecue spot, with band.
Trattoria Romantica, 13 Evagoras Pallikarides St., tel. 02-465276, is a good Italian restaurant.
The Indian Restaurant, 45 Prodromos St., tel. 02-452183, is open 12am-2.30pm and 7-11pm; closed on Sunday. A choice of 50 traditional Indian entrées.

Pizza Parlours
Pizza Palace: 2 Aeschylus St., Makedonidissa.
Pizzarama: 2 Michael Karaoli St., Engomi.

Shopping
The main shopping centre in the old city is on Ledra St., a narrow alley ending at an army post, on the Green Line. The street is lined with a series of small shops, with

Laiki Yitonia

a rather poor selection of clothing and electronics, but with some quite good footwear outlets. There are several handicraft shops, selling copper, silver, earthenware and even lace.

For more attractive shop windows, stroll along Evagoras Ave., where you will even find *Benetton*, *Stefanel*, *Woolworth* and *Marks and Spenser* outlets.

At the corner of Dhigeni Akrita and Theodotou Sts., south-east of the old city, you will find the open market. Near the access road to the Limassol highway, on Athalassa Ave., there's an arts-and-crafts centre on your left.

Entertainment
Most entertainment spots are in Laiki Yitonia and west of the centre, along George Grivas Ave.

Behind the *Ledra* hotel there is a ten-lane bowling alley, always very crowded on weekends. Not far from there is the Nicosia International Fair grounds.

In Engomi, slightly more than a mile from the centre, there are two discos: *Africana Disco* (1a Michali Paridi St., tel. 02-456495, open nightly), and *Scorpios Disco* (3 Stassinos St., tel. 02-445967), the oldest of all Cyprus' discos.

The **Town Theatre** is very central, near Museum St.; all performances are in Greek.

Young people mostly frequent the Eleftheria Sq. pubs, but are also happy to stroll along the main shopping areas.

Sports
Six miles south-west of Nicosia there is a Sports Centre and a riding school.

Races are held regularly at Agios Dhometios, one of Nicosia's suburbs, one mile east of the town centre. Racing events are held on Sunday (June and July on Saturday); no races from mid-July to mid-September. The address of the *Nicosia Racing Club* is P.O.B 1783, Nicosia.

Tennis courts are available at most hotels, and also: *Champs Elisées:* tel. 02-457088; two asphalt courts. *Eleon*

Tennis Club: 3 Ploutarchous St., Engomi, tel. 02-449923, 2 dirt courts and 7 asphalt courts.

Fairs and Festivals
The annual Nicosia international fair is held on the last week of May. In September there is an arts festival.

What to See
We will start our walk from **Laiki Yitonia**, the restored quarter within the old city. It is the pride of all Nicosians and the centre of the capital's night and day life. Restoration began in 1981, and included renewal and reconstruction of all structures within the target area. Now the streets are lined with small art-and-crafts shows, boutiques and galleries. The project won the 1988 "Pomme d'Or", a prestigious biennial international prize.

After a leisurely stroll, find your way to the **Leventis Municipal Museum** (at 17 Hippocrates St.). The building is a characteristic mansion dating from the end of the 19th century, very accurately restored. It houses an interesting presentation of Nicosia's daily life throughout the ages. Open Tuesday-Sunday, 10am-4.30pm. Free entrance.

An evening visit to the quarter is also highly recommended: surrender to the pleas of one of the restaurant waiters, sit and enjoy the sight, your *meze* and the *bouzuki* band.

To visit the sites of the old city in the eastern quarter, leave Laiki Yitonia, and follow Constantinos Paleologos and Nikoforos Aves. along the inner side of the wall. After some 500 yards you will find yourself at the **Liberty Monument**, on the corner of Nikoforos and Koraes Sts. The monument commemorates the release of EOKA Cyprian patriots in 1959.

Turn left into Koraes St., following it to the Kyprianos and Zenon of Kitium Sts. corner.

Between these two streets you will find several interesting structures and sites. The first, to the south is the **Archbishopric Palace**, a modern (1955-60) mansion,

The Liberty Monument

built in Byzantine style. It is an impressive mansion, whose extravagance may even appear shocking and inappropriate, in view of the poverty so clearly evident in some of the capital's slums.

Further north is the **Agios Ioannis Cathedral** (Greek Orthodox). Built in 1662 on the foundations of a 15th century Benedictine Monastery, its impressive interiors house a series of reproductions of 18th century works of art. The most magnificent is the *Judgement Day*, you will find it above the southern door.

Cross the inner court of St. John's Cathedral, and enter the **Cultural Centre of the Archbishop Makarios III Foundation**. The Centre houses the **Byzantine Museum**, with a collection of statues, paintings and fragments from a period ranging from the 8th to the 18th century. It depicts the development of the decorative arts in Cyprus from their crudest Early Middle Age

The statue of Archbishop Makarios III in front of
the Archbishopric Palace

expression to their 12th century peak. The influence of European Crusaders, and later of Venetian traders, is evident. During the Ottoman period (16th-19th centuries) the figurative arts, and specially sculpture, were neglected and practically abandoned.

The museum is open May-September, Monday-Friday, 9.30am-1pm and 2-5.30pm (Saturday 9am-1pm); the rest of the year, Monday-Friday 9am-1pm and 2-5pm (Saturday 9am-1pm).

Further north on Cyprianos St., you will find two other museums on your left. The first is the **Museum of the National Struggle**, dedicated to the war of independence against the British (open Monday-Friday, 7.30am-1.30pm and 3-5pm, Saturday 7.30am-1.30pm; the rest of the year Monday-Friday 7.30am-2pm, 3-5pm, Saturday 7.30am- 1pm). Entrance fee.

The next is a 15th century Benedictine monastery, housing the **Museum of Folk Art**. Its halls contain a collection of Benedictine relics, ancient farming tools, religious art objects, *Lefkaritika* and other lace and Foini earthenware.

The museum is open Monday-Friday, 8.30am-1pm and 2-6pm; Saturday mornings only. Entrance fee.

West of the old city, near the Pafos Gate, inside the City Gardens, is the **Cyprus Museum** (Stylianos Lenas Sq., corner of Museum St. and Homer Ave.). Walk along Homer Ave., outside the walls, from Eleftheria Sq. until you reach Stylianos Lenas Sq.

Built in 1908, the Cyprus Museum is the most important archaeological museum on the island. It contains stone jars of the 6th millennium AC (from Choirokoitia), a marble statue of Aphrodites (from Soli, 1st century BC) and a gold sceptre (from Kourion, 11th century BC). Open Monday-Saturday, 9am-5pm, Sunday 10am-1pm.

Across the square are the **Botanic Gardens**, with an interesting collection of flowers, shrubs and trees.

The **Cyprus Handicraft Centre** is at 25 Demophontos St. It houses a permanent collection of handicrafts as well as a handicraft sales centre.

The **Museum of Modern Arts** is at the corner of Evagorou and Themistokli Dervi Aves.; open June-September, Monday-Friday, 10am-1pm and 4-7pm, Saturday 10am-1pm; the rest of the year Monday-Friday 10am-1pm and 3-6pm, Saturday 10an-1pm.

Around Nicosia

Tamassos

Leave Nicosia south-westward on the main road to Kato Lakatameia and Kato Deftera. Follow it until the Pera turnoff (on the right-hand side). Cross Pera and proceed to Episkopeion. Here turn left to Politikon. Before reaching this last village you will see the Tamassos archaeological site on your left.

In ancient times, Tamassos was one of Cyprus' main centres, surrounded by fertile farmland and rich copper mines. Its two main temples were dedicated to Apollo and Aphrodite. In the course of the 1970's, the site was mapped and researched, bringing to light the foundations of several large structures and important fragments from the Sanctuary of Aphrodite. Not far from the site are also two burial caves discovered in 1890 (a third cave was completely destroyed). These caves have been assigned to the 7th century BC, and are relatively well preserved. The first and wider one contains a reconstructed porch and two burial rooms. The porch roof is supported by two columns decorated with Greek inscriptions. The ceilings are almost 8 feet tall, and the size of the rooms is approximately 9x10 feet. The second cave is similar to the first, only slightly smaller.

The site is open to visitors June-September, Tuesday-Sunday, 9-12am and 4-7pm; the rest of the year, 9am-1pm and 2-4.30pm; also closed on Monday. Entrance fee.

The Athalassa National Park
This is a 10 mile ride (by car or by bicycle). Leave Nicosia toward Limassol, but turn left at the highway entrance traffic lights. The road will take you to a pleasant park of pine, eucalyptus and cedar trees. If you secured a permit in advance (tel. 02-403526 — at the cost of CYP1), you may stop and fish along the dam.

Dhali
Leave Nicosia toward Limassol, either on the highway or on the old Limassol Road. Nine miles off Nicosia, take the left-hand turnoff to **Dhali**, a village built on the ruins of the ancient site of **Idalion**, on the southern side of the Valias river. According to myth, Idalion was founded by Khalcanor, one of the heroes of the Trojan war, who built 14 sanctuaries to Aphrodite, Apollo, Athena and other gods in his new citadel.

The first survey of the site was carried out in 1865-1876 by the American consul Luigi Palma de Chensola, who discovered literally thousands of tombs, most of which are presently housed at the **New York City Museum**. These findings date to the 12th century BC, but lower and earlier levels were later discovered, going back to the 17th century BC. Later, excavations also uncovered fragments of the 6th and 7th century BC city walls, as well as hundreds of coins, fragments and artifacts of the Aechean, Hellenistic and Roman periods.

Useful Addresses and Telephones
Nicosia prefix: 02.
Police, first aid and fire brigade: tel. 199.
Hospital: Homer Ave., tel. 445111.
Municipality: Constantinos Paleologos Ave., near Eleftheria Sq.
CTO: Laiki Yitonia, tel. 444264.
British Embassy: 36 Alexander Pallis St., tel. 02-471311
USA Embassy: corner of Dositheos and Therissos Sts., tel. 02-465151.
German Embassy: 10 Nikitaras St., tel. 02-444362.
Swedish Embassy: Princess Zena de Tyra Palace, tel. 02-442483.
Norwegian Embassy: 4 Metaxakis St., tel. 02-472024.

Turkish Cyprus

Lefkosa — Turkish Nicosia

Crossing to the Turkish side

One may also visit the **TRNC (Turkish Republic of Northern Cyprus)**. This requires crossing the "Green Line", which is regularly patrolled by the United Nations Peace Corps.

Proceed to the Pafos Gate, with your valid passport in hand. The first thing you will see is a huge wall billboard, beckoning the tourist to visit the dilapidated and empty homes and the ruined sanctuaries — and never to forget 1974. Your name will be registered at the border control and you will be asked to reenter the Greek zone by 5pm (when the gate closes). Now you will be asked to proceed to the Ledra Palace (today the UN Peace Corps barracks and border post. On the mansion walls you will see the signs of dozens of old bullet holes. On the Turkish side you will be asked to fill in another form, to pay 1CYP and to present your passport.

One of the waiting taxis will take you to the centre of Lefkosa or to any other site in Turkish Cyprus — such as Kyrenia for example. The centre of Lefkosa is less than a mile away, within easy walking distance.

A visit to Lefkosa will only take a few hours. In this chapter we will take you through its main (not very well preserved) sites, to the marketplace and to a pleasant and inexpensive lunch.

You may cross the border with your car (a special insurance policy can be purchased at the gate), but we recommend the simpler alternatives of a taxi ride or walk. If you plan a visit to other Turkish Cyprus sites, you should cross the border in the early morning: the gate opens at 8am and you must be back before 5pm. Failure to do so will automatically put you on the "missing persons" list, with all the unpleasant formalities this entails.

The local currency is the Turkish Pound, but CYP, $US and European currencies are always welcome.

Only tourists are admitted to Turkish Cyprus; the border is absolutely closed to Greek Cypriots.

What to See

Lefkosa is a rather sorry sight. Its alleys are neglected and untidy; the houses are unattractive. Independence, apparently, did not bring prosperity to Turkish Cyprus: it brought neglect and isolation.

The **Turkish Museum** (a.k.a. Mevlevi Tekke) is near the Kyrenia Gate, in an early 17th century building, a former Dervish sanctuary.

In the **Berbers' Museum** you will find enough evidence of the continuous feud between Turkish and Greek Cypriots. The museum was the former family residence of Major Ilhan, who was killed in 1963 by EOKA fighters. Ilhan was a major in the Army Medical Corps — the medical officer of one of the Turkish battalions. After his death he became a symbol of the Turkish struggle.

The **Selimiye Mosque** was built as the St. Sophie Cathedral in the de Lusignans period (13th century), in French Gothic style fashionable at the time. It was a joint project of Queen Alix de Champagne and of Archbishop Thiryx. After its consecration, it was used for the coronation ceremonies of the de Lusignan kings. The Ottoman conquerors transformed it into a mosque, adding three minarets to it and an offering table. However, the 14th century statues and reliefs of saints and angels on its doors and panels have survived, even if the mosque is used daily for Moslem rituals.

Near the mosque you will see the **Bedesten** (= bazaar),

a trade and handicraft centre, set up by the Ottoman conquerors in what used to be St. Nicholas of the English, a 14th century Greek Orthodox church, very popular during the Venetian period.

The **Lapidary Museum** is a 15th century Venetian building.

In the **Sultan Mahmoud II's Library**, built in 1829 by the Turk Governor Al Ruhi, you will find thousands of volumes from the great Sultan's private library. On the window sill of the small reading room you will see the Sultan's crest and signature. The library also contains later book donations, side by side with the original library of Mahmoud II.

The **Obelisk** was brought to Lefkosa from Salamis; it commemorates the Venetian conquest of Cyprus in the 15th century.

The **Büyük Han** (= Great Inn) and the **Kumarcılar Han** (= Gamblers' Inn) are two neighbouring and very similar Ottoman structures. The first is, of course, slightly larger and also older. It has an inner court for carriages, with a small mosque in its centre.

Tours in Turkish Cyprus

Two brief tours of Turkish Cyprus are outlined in the following itineraries; westward and eastward from the capital. Both tours start from Lefkosa and pass through Girne (Kyrenia). Each of the tours requires at leat one full day, but we recommend an overnight stop. Nevertheless, tourists arriving through the Nicosia Pafos Gate are advised to cut their tour short, in order to re-enter Greek Nicosia before 5pm.

The Western Tour

The itinerary: Lefkosa — Girne — the western coast — Güzelyurt (Morphou in Greek) — Lefke — Nicosia. Total: little more than 100 miles.

Leave Lefkosa northward on the Kyrenia road; on the

Selimiye Mosque

way you will pass the villages of Ortaköy and Gönyeli, and cross the Kyrenia Range (in Turkish Beşparmak). Ten miles off Lefkosa, on the pass, turn left to the **Agios Ilarion Castle** (little more than one mile from the road). This castle is the best preserved of three Medieval fortresses situated along the Kyrenia Range (the others are the Kantara and the Buffavento Castles). It was built in the 10th century as the St. Ilarion Monastery, but was subsequently buttressed and transformed into a fortress. Today the old monastery is in ruins, but within its walls there is a relatively well-preserved 11th century Byzantine church. The battlements are armed with 9 turrets. Among the monastery ruins you will recognize the monks' quarters, the cellars, the summer residence of the de Lusignan family and St. Ilarion's tomb. Near the regal suite of the de Lusignans you will see a narrow building, whose styles reflect different periods.

Back to the main road, turn left, and after 3 more miles you will arrive in Kyrenia.

Kyrenia
Before the 1974 war, this town used to be one of Cyprus' major tourist resorts, thanks to its excellent strategic position, in the centre of Cyprus' northern coastline and at the foot of the Kyrenia Range. Its hotels still remain, but are mostly deserted.

Kyrenia's first settlements date from 6,000 years ago. It is an archaeologist's paradise, with scores of sites to explore and dozens of mountain groves and sunny beaches to spend leisure time.

The Sites
The Venetians determined the present rectangular shape of the **Girne Castle** (remember: Girne-Kyrenia). It served as their first defensive stronghold against the Ottoman threat. The Venetians built it on an old Byzantine fort, designed to check the 7th century wave of Arab expansion. You may enter through the modern bridge, from which a long corridor will take you to a section of the fort dating from the de Lusignan period (14th century).

*C*YPRUS

You may also enter the fort through a passage situated at the tomb of the Turkish admiral Sadık Paşa.

Today the fort houses Kyrenia's **Sailing Ships Museum**. Here you will find the remains of one of the most ancient boats ever recovered from the bottom of the sea. It dates back to the 4th century BC, sunk in the Kyrenia Bay, one mile off the harbour, at the time of Alexander the Great. You will also see part of the merchandise found in its holds, including 4,000 wine amphoras, scores of wooden tools, four oil amphoras and four salt containers, etc.

The **Museum of Arts** exhibits a collection of European modern art, various objects from the Far East, and Chinese and European porcelain.

The **Museum of Folk Art** is housed within a splendid residence, characteristic of the better class of 18th century Cypriots. The mansion is situated at the Kyrenia harbour, and it has three main levels. Its cellars were used as a storing area. The first floor was the services, kitchen and crafts area; now it exhibits a collection of farming tools and looms. The second floor was the living area; the third was the bedroom's floor, and here you will find a selection of home furnishing dating back to this period including, bedcloths, tablecloths, local embroidery and lace, as well as a collection of gold and silver objects.

Not far from the harbour you will find the mosque of **Cafer Paşa**, with its tall minaret — a splendid example of Ottoman architecture.

Around Kyrenia
About 6 miles east of Kyrenia you will find the **Belapais Abbey**, a 12th century monastery in the Gothic style of the de Lusignan period. The monastery is built around an inner court, where the church, the dining room and the dormitory of the monks are located. It is also known as the **Blanche Abbey**, (Blanche-White in French), probably because of the white habit worn by its monks. The monastery was erected by the Order of St. Norbert, one of the less known orders of the Middle Ages.

The building is very well preserved, and its dining room

(30x90 feet), built by King Hugh IV, is one of the best examples of Cyprus' Gothic style. Several first rank figures of Cyprus' history are supposed to be buried here, but their tombs have not yet been found. Above the entrance door you will see the crest of the de Lusignans. From the six windows of the northern wall you will enjoy a splendid view of the sea, framed by the Taurus peaks, in the Anatolian Peninsula.

West of Kyrenia

After this brief visit to Kyrenia, follow the coastal road westward, toward **Güzelyurt**. After 12 miles the road turns left (south), crossing the village of Panagra, where you will see the road sign indicating Güzelyurt, a small town in the midst of Cyprus' famous lemon groves.

Güzelyurt means "beautiful land", and this small provincial town is indeed situated on one of Cyprus' most beautiful spots, whose fertile soil is covered in citrus groves and vineyards and blessed with endless freshwater springs. The produce of the lemon groves is mainly for export, either in fruit form or as bottled juice. The town itself has no major tourist sites; it ows its charm exclusively to nature. It has some attractive beaches, and even some casinos.

Proceed south-westward, crossing Prastion to the archaeological site of Soli and to the Vouni Palace. After 9 miles you will come to the town of **Lefke**, another fertile enclave not far from the Güzelyurt Bay. Near Lefke there is one of Cyprus' old copper mines. North of Lefke, very near the coastal road, is the Archaeological Site of **Soli**.

Soli was founded in the 6th century BC by King Philohypros, whose adviser was none other than Solon of Athens. Only a few decades later the town fell, after a long siege, into Persian hands. Soli's best period was under Rome. The town was completely destroyed in 648 by the Arabs. As in other sites, the ruins served as building blocks for construction of another town — in this case Port Said, in Egypt (in the 19th century). The site was researched for the first time in 1929; the first,

Lefkosa

The Bedesten — used to be St. Nicolas Church

Agios Ilarion Castle

clamorous finding was a Roman amphitheatre with 17 rows of seats, a semi-circular chorus and a rectangular stage. The acropolis was uncovered several years later, together with the mosaic floor of a very early church.

Having visited Soli, proceed westward for 3 miles along the coastal road and you will come to the **Vouni Palace**, enclosed within a brick wall on the top of an 800 feet high hill. The palace was built in the 5th century BC, at the approximate time of the great Cypriot rebellion against the Persians. The building was erected by the town governor of Merion, to prevent further armed attacks by the Cypriot rebels. A few years later a **Temple of Athena** was erected on the palace grounds, together with a series of ancillar buildings: residences, kitchens, storerooms, and barracks. In total, the palace had no less than 147 rooms.

While the outer wall was made of bricks, the palace walls were made of stone. Most of the palace was destroyed by fire in the year 380, and it was never rebuilt.

Back to Nicosia

Leaving the Vouni Palace, you will start out on your way back to Lefkosa, and through the Pafos Gate to Greek Nicosia. Follow the coast of the Güzelyurt Bay, crossing Güzelyurt itself; the main road from here to Nicosia crosses the border between Turkish and Greek Cyprus, and therefore it is closed to traffic. The alternative route is somewhat longer and not in the best possible condition. Three miles north of Güzelyurt on the Kyrenia road, in the vicinity of Kapouti (in Greek Kalon Chorion), turn right (eastward), passing through Skylloura and make your way toward Nicosia.

The distance from the capital is 13 miles at the most, but the unavoidable detours that must be made to avoid crossing the border will take you further north to Agios Ermalaos and, after 6 more miles, to Krini and to the Kyrenia-Nicosia main road. Just six more miles, and you will arrive in Nicosia.

C YPRUS

The Eastern Tour

The itinerary: Lefkosa — Famagusta (Gazi Maguza in Turkish) — Salamis — the Karpas Peninsula — the Kantara Fortress — Kyrenia (Girne) — Nicosia is approximately 125 miles.

Leave Lefkosa eastward on the main road to Famagusta. Take the northern route (the southern route crosses into Greek Cyprus territory, and therefore is closed to Famagusta traffic). The road crosses the rather flat and uninteresting Mesaoria plain, and after about 36 miles you will reach Famagusta.

Famagusta

Before 1974 Famagusta (for the Turks, Gazi Magusa), was the best known name in Cyprus, thanks to its deep-water harbour, its very well sheltered marina and the hotels lining the beach. Since 1974, Famagusta belongs to Turkish Cyprus, and the town has fallen into ruin. It stopped growing, tourists stopped coming, its hotels fell into disrepair; only the major historic sites have kept most of their appeal.

Famagusta has a very rich history, indeed the richest in all of Cyprus. It began as a small fishermen's harbour, but during the de Lusignan period it became the island's main port-of-call, with hundreds of ships anchoring there on the way to Europe, to the Holy Land and to the East.

The sites

The **St. Nicholas Cathedral** was built in 1298 by the de Lusignans. It is undoubtedly one of the most impressive and best preserved churches in Cyprus. Several Kings of Cyprus (and of Jerusalem) were crowned in this church. When the Ottomans conquered the town from the Venetians, in 1571, the cathedral was transformed into a mosque, equipped with a minaret and an offering table, and renamed Lâla Mustafa Paşa. It remains a mosque to this day.

The so-called **Venetian Walls** also belong to the de Lusignan period. They are 2.5 miles long and enclose the

Kyrenia — near the port

entire old city. Originally the walls were more than 6 feet thick, and they were equipped with several turrets. When artillery made its appearance, in 1489, the Venetians decided to strengthen the walls, until they were 60 feet tall and more than 20 feet thick. On the outside a moat was dug, and kept full of water at all times. There were two entrance gates, that could be crossed through a drawbridge. However, even that was insufficient to save Famagusta from the Turks, who after four months of bitter fighting conquered it in 1571.

The **Othello Castle** is a second defensive fort, built by the de Lusignans in the 13th century. Again, after 1492 the Venetians added new thickness to its walls and expanded it as well. According to legend, this is where

The port

Cristoforo Moro, a high Venetian official in Cyprus during the years 1506-08, killed his beautiful but unfaithful wife Desdemona. As you undoubtedly know, the news also reached Shakespeare. Hence, the present name of the Castle.

The old **Church of the Sts. Peter and Paul**, built in 1358, became the Sinan Paşa Mosque during the Ottoman period. Çelebi Mehmet Efendi, a Turkish diplomat of the 18th century,is buried in its court. After serving as his Sultan's ambassador in France he retired to Cyprus and died here in 1732.

The **Namık Kemal Prison** bears the name of a famous poet, imprisoned here from 1873-76 by the Sultan Abdul

Aziz. Originally the palace was one of the royal residences of the de Lusignans. It was looted by the Turks in 1571, and its ruins were later restored as a police post and a prison.

The **Canbolat Museum** contains an ethnographic collection of objects recovered in the town and its district. It bears the name of Canbolat Bey, a Turkish hero, who fell in battle while defending the city, he is buried in the museum grounds.

Salamis

Salamis, 4 miles north of Famagusta, is one of the most important archaeological sites on the island. The site of **Alasia**, one of Cyprus' most ancient settlements, is also in the same area.

Leave Famagusta on the Engomi road, along the coast. After 3 miles, turn left toward Engomi and Alasia. Alasia was an affluent settlement during the Bronze Age. Its name is mentioned in several Egyptian papyri. Archaeologists found gold and ivory ornaments, amphoras and Mycaenean earthenware in several of the tombs.

Proceed further on, and after little more than half a mile turn right, toward the seashore. Having reached the coastal road, turn left for less than a mile, and you will see the site of **Salamis** on your right.

Salamis' mythological father is Tefkros, another hero of the Trojan War, banned by his father, King of Salamis, who blamed him for the suicide of his brother Ajax. Tefkros landed, at what used to be known as the Akalar Beach, with a handful of faithful followers. As soon as he settled down, he built a temple to Zeus (whose ruins can be seen to this day in the southern section of the market,) and gave his town the name of his childhood home, Salamis.

The town had an inner and an outer wall; fragments of the **inner wall** can be seen at the entrance of town. An earthquake in the 4th century destroyed most of the buildings; the ruins of the Roman Amphitheatre were later used to build the **Turkish Baths**. The **amphitheatre**, with its spacious stage, can still be clearly identified. Along the stage you can see the trench used to collect blood from the victims consecrated to Dyonisos before each ritual. Only the first eight of the fifty rows of seats belong to the original Roman structure; the rest are much later additions. In the *agora* (market place) a memorial stone bears witness to its inauguration, in the year 22 BC.

The Karpas Peninsula

Follow the main coastal road toward the north; after 9 miles, near Bogazi, you will come to the tip of the Karpas Peninsula, a long and narrow strip of hilly farmland pointing toward east-north-east. It is a region full of water sources; and its sea-water teams with fish and other seafood. You will also find several hot-water springs on the peninsula as well as the **Kantara Castle** and the Apostolos Andreas Monastery. All this does not change the fact that this is one of the most deserted regions on the island.

The road proceeds along the peninsula well beyond Bogazi, for 36 miles, and ends at **Cape Andreas**, with the **Apostolos Andreas Monastery** and a lonely lighthouse. Those who were short of time will have turned north at Bogazi, taking the mountain road that climbs the Beşparmak Range ("Five Fingers"), then turning right to stop briefly at the Kantara Castle.

The **Kantara Castle** is the last of the three fortresses built during the Byzantine period on top of the Kyrenia Range. It towers over the coastal strip from a height of 2000 feet. It is almost inaccessible, and even after centuries of wars, during which it often changed hands, its walls and ramparts still remain almost perfectly preserved.

Proceeding westward and then northward from Kantara, you will reach the little town of Davlos, and the main coastal road. Follow it westward to **Belapais** and to the **Belapais Monastery**, familiar from "The Western Tour". From here, the road continues to Kyrenia, and from here

View from Belapais Abbey

you will turn back to Lefkosa and to the Pafos Gate to Greek Nicosia.

*I*NDEX

A

Agia Napa..65
Agios Hermogenis...90
Agios Ilarion Castle...147
Agios Trias Church..74
Agros...89, 121
Akrotiri...88
Alasia...156
Alassa..88
Alona..120
Amathous..77
Angeloktistos Church..64
Apostolos Andreas Monastery...............................157
Arsos..109
Athalassa National Park..141
Ayia Thekla...72

B

Baths of Aphrodite..108
Belapais Abbey...148, 157
Bogazi...157
Buffavento Castle..147

C

Cape Andreas...157
Cape Arnaoutis...108
Cape Greco...74
Cape Drepanon...107
Caledonia Falls...123
Chandria...121
Choirokoitia..77
Chrisochou Bay...108
Coral Bay..107
Curium..90

D

Dhali...141

E

Episkopi..90
Erimi...89

INDEX

F

Famagusta 153
Fig Tree Bay 73
Flamingo Bay 73
Foini 89, 109, 118

G

Galata 119
Gereskipou 94, 105
Germasogia Dam 88
Girne Castle 147
Golden Sands 73
Güzelyurt 149

H

Hala Sultan Tekke Mosque 64

I

Idalion 141

K

Kalopanagiotis 118
Kalon Chorion 89
Kakopetria 113
Kantara 147
Kantara Castle 157
Karpas Peninsula 157
Kato Lefkara 76
Kato Platres 89
Kolossi 89
Kolossi Castle 90
Kouklia 93
Kourion 90
Ktima 104
Kykkos Monastery 109, 118
Kyperounta 113, 120
Kyrenia 147

L

Lagoudera 120
Lara Bay 107
Larnaca 53, 129
Larnaca Salt Lake 63
Lefkara 76
Lefke 149
Lefkosa 143
Limassol 79

INDEX

Linou..119
Lower Pafos...101

M
Machairas Monastery..120
Makronisos..72
Merion...152
Moutoullas...118
Mt. Olympus..121

N
Nicosia...125
Nikitari...124
Nikokleia...109
Nissi..72

O
Omodos..89, 109

P
Palaia Pafos..93
Palaichori..120
Palodeia..89
Pamboula..64
Panagia Angeloktistos..64
Panagia Chrysopantanassa..120
Pano Lefkara...76
Pano Panagia..109
Pano Platres..89
Pafos..95
Pafos Gate..129
Paralimni...74
Pedoulas..116, 118
Pegeia...107
Petra tou Romiou...93
Platanistasa...120
Polis...108
Prastion..109
Prodromos...118
Protaras..74
Pyla...64, 89

S
Stavrovouni Monastery..76
Salamis...156
Sandy Beach...72
Soli...149
Sotira..92

*I*NDEX

T

Tamassos...124, 140
Troodhitissa Monastery...118
Troodos..112
Troodos Mountains...88, 112
Tombs of the Kings...104

V

Vouni Palace...152

NOTES

NOTES

NOTES

NOTES

QUESTIONNAIRE

In our efforts to keep up with the pace and pulse of Cyprus, we kindly ask your cooperation in sharing with us any information which you may have as well as your comments. We would greatly appreciate your completing and returning the following questionnaire. Feel free to add additional pages. A complimentary copy of the next edition will be sent to you should any of your suggestions be included.

Our many thanks!

To: Inbal Travel Information (1983) Ltd.
18 Hayetzira Street
Ramat Gan 52521
Israel

Name: _____

Address: _____

_____

Occupation: _____

Date of visit: _____

_____

Purpose of trip (vacation, business, etc.): _____

_____

_____

Comments/Information: _____

_____

_____

_____

_____

_____

_____

_____

_____

_____

_____

_____

_____

_____

_____

INBAL Travel Information Ltd.
P.O.B. 39090 Tel Aviv
ISRAEL 61390